Endorsements for *A Walker Trilogy*

"*Under the Firefly Moon* wonderfully interwoven between deep love for storytelling and reading, family summertime, and adventurous spirit is a must read for all ages." by Tony Landon McGregor, PhD.

As a friend and co-worker with Dr. Daisy A. Palmer for many years, her family history story-telling continually provided amusement and inspiration—such as the story of her pet skunk on the farm in the "good-ole-days." You have seen the episodes of "I Love Lucy"; now, you can laugh, cry, and share true-to-life experiences and very inspirational stories from a remarkable family, as provided by Dr. Palmer, The remarkable and detailed recollection of her family's history of daily survival and inspiration family achievements provides priceless memories, which will be forever treasured.

Dr. Palmer provides inspirational family memories of making wild plum pudding; getting water with a dipper from the water well; milking the cows; traveling across a river in the covered wagon with all your possessions; family Bible reading; going through goat-head thorns to get melons; visits from the ice delivery man; following the bees to find honey; making quilts for the family; writing poems; proper way to noodle for catfish; family songs with harmonicas, guitars, etc.; repairing and inventing machinery; dealing with death, sickness, and daily provisions for the family; cooking mountain oysters, which is not sea food—and, frog legs; playing jacks, jump rope, and family games; canned goods in the cellar with the rats; appreciation of good ole fried chicken; and, chores of daily feeding the hogs and chickens.

In the story *Under the Firefly Moon*, see how the girls had glowing rings on their fingers. Hint: Had something to do with homemade ice cream and lots of fireflies in the yard. Also, Dr. Palmer provides very inspirational stories and facts on the military achievements with the family.

Today, Dr. Daisy Palmer is still spreading inspiration with her wonderful story-telling and interaction with people. Her beloved mother was deaf; therefore, Dr. Palmer became very proficient in lip-reading and the use of American Sign Language. As a part of her inspirational journey in life, she serves as the Vice President for the American Foundation for the Elderly Deaf, Inc.(AFED) and to be President of AFED in January 2014 So, pull out a chair! Get ready for some very inspirational writing by Dr. Palmer. By G. L. Cook, President, Peace on Earth International Evangelistic Association

A Walker Trilogy
Three to Read on Walker Mountain

Daisyann Walker Palmer, PhD

Inspiring Voices®
A Service of **Guideposts**

Inspiring Voices books may be ordered through booksellers or by contacting:

Inspiring Voices
1663 Liberty Drive
Bloomington, IN 47403
www.inspiringvoices.com
1-(866) 697-5313

Because of the dynamic nature of the Internet, any web addresses or links contained in this book may have changed since publication and may no longer be valid. The views expressed in this work are solely those of the author and do not necessarily reflect the views of the publisher, and the publisher hereby disclaims any responsibility for them.

Any people depicted in stock imagery provided by Thinkstock are models, and such images are being used for illustrative purposes only.

Certain stock imagery © Thinkstock.

ISBN: 978-1-4624-0742-2 (sc)
ISBN: 978-1-4624-0743-9 (e)

Library of Congress Control Number: 2013949741

Printed in the United States of America.

Inspiring Voices rev. date: 10/07/2013

Table of Contents

Acknowledegement vii

Dedication ix

Boys Searching for Melons 1

Under the Firefly Moon 17

Wheels: Mechanical, Music, Story, Cookie, Poetry, Soldier 43

Documentation Appendix 57

Epilogue 63

Acknowlededegement

The story telling began as a child entertaining my brother, Leroy E. Walker II. Then cousins wanted stories read. Next, while traveling with daughters Christy and Cyndi, telling stories made them forget to ask, "Are we there yet?" Stories told to grandchildren Jason, Starla, Justin caused them to ask for more family tales. Stories shared with nieces Christina and Heather introduced them to their Grandfather and Great Grandfather. Recently discovered cousins, Rosalyn, Carolyn, June, Emory, and Andrea, are constantly reminding me the Walker Stories need telling. Cousins to meet Gary and Bobby, appear in story dreams. Cousins always kin seeking as in Janice, Alvena, Jeanette, Helen, and Rosemary insist a Walker Mountain is among their searching. The DAR cousin Nelda, while in the other family tree, allows no rest for the weary researcher. Sharron, the cousin more of a sister, and willing to go in two covered wagons (one wagon for a wooden bath tub for bubble baths under the stars big and bright at night and other wagon for food and clothes) to discover family tales, thank you greatly for the giggles, jack games, hopscotch, and jump rope games. Thank you, special friend, John for constant encouragement and saying, "Tell me a story."

Grandfather, Great Spirit, all over the world the faces of living things are alike. With tenderness, they have come up out of the ground. Look upon your children that they may face the winds and walk the good road to the days of quiet. Grandfather, Great Spirit, fill us with the light, give us strength to understand and the eyes to see, teach us to walk the soft earth as relatives to all that live. Black Elk Prayer

Dedication

Bygone Walkers living well their life stories

Present Day Walkers Emory, Gary, Bobby,
Leroy II, Leroy III
WWW (Wild Walker Women) too numerous
to list.

Future Walkers sharing, adding to, and preserving life stories

Supreme tributes bestowed to Walker Men preserving sovereignty for USA through the Constitution for the freedom of speech to share stories.

WWI Lawrence Ezra Walker, Corporal, Louis Floyd Walker, PVT
WWII Lytle Reese Walker, Jr., 2nd LT., Lawrence Hall Walker Fireman 2nd Class
Korean Emory Clair Walker, Jr., 2nd LT, Purple Heart
Vietnam Dr. RJ Black Henson, Colonel, Treating Casualties, Marvin Zane Walker, Major, 19 air medals and 2 Distinguished Flying Crosses

May all never forget what is worth remembering or ever remember what is best forgotten.   Irish Wisdom

Boys Searching for Melons

The land rush of Oklahoma brought sad times and heavy memories for Lawrence C. and Rosa M. (Klopfenstein) Walker. Their first-born daughter died of the dreaded thrush and was hastily buried in a pioneer cemetery before counties were established in Oklahoma. They were hoping for a new start with new memories in a soon to be new state, but the loss of their first daughter Clisty Jane, a month old infant, was due to unavailable medical care during in the 1892 land rush. On a bone chilling January day in 1893, the diminutive mother Rosa sadly gave the entire delicate baby girl's clothing to a relative. She did not know she was newly with child, another girl to be born in the autumn of 1893.

This girl, named Vernie, traveled the summer 1906 journey of the new century to Quay County, New Mexico. She, at thirteen, saw exciting adventures filled with girl cousins for companions. She would carry none of her parents' melancholy in her heart or her pockets for that matter. Instead, she carried hair ribbons for her cousins in her pockets. She could hardly wait to meet up with her female cousins Effie and Fairy Pamelia. She knew of Fairy's writing talents and could barely contain her excitement to read some of her cousin's poems and short stories. One of Fairy's poems was hand written in her mother's bible. Vernie had committed it to memory and recited it daily.

True Contentment

By Fairy Walker

Four walls can hold contentment,
Dear home where love and peace abide;
Containing life's richest treasures,
Wherever we go, or what betide.

Vernie knew bringing hair ribbons all the way from Kansas would endear her to Walker cousins she had never met. Little did she know that Fairy would become a proficient published writer. Some of those compositions are in this trilogy of stories about the Walker family adventures.

Vernie watched her parents carry their miseries like heavy stones tearing holes in their hearts. Secretly, she had prayed for a baby sister to prove her Mother could have more than her four brothers: Lethron, Leroy, Gladstone, and Joseph. Fairy Vivian, the baby sister, was Vernie's answered prayers.

The parents were loading all their possessions into the covered wagon in the spring of 1906. Their thoughts to acquire land in the New Mexico territory near their eldest son working for the Southern Pacific Railroad were foremost in their minds. They hoped their second son could find work alongside his brother. The money the boys brought home would be for corn seed beans, melons and other fine crops for water was plentiful. Putting aside money for the hard times was part of their plans.

The mother's sadness was complicated in that her eldest son, Lethron, known as Leck, had signed on with the Southern Pacific Railroad. His saying he would prepare for her a dugout house did not soothe her aching heart. Little did she know he had taken a job finding water wells for the Southern Pacific Railroad. Leck found a spring fed well in 1905 that would survive well into the next century serving the needs of railroads and humans alike.

Rosa felt as if her children were disappearing. She never recovered from the loss of her first daughter Clisty Jane buried in an unknown grave in Oklahoma. Then her dear mother Sarah Jane Kirk Klopfenstein had passed suddenly in 1904 at Berlin, Oklahoma the last homestead of her family. She was unable to travel to the funeral for railroads did not yet reach the far western lands of Oklahoma. The ten or more days by wagon were unthinkable. Rosa was hoping the family would stop on this trip so she could at least see her mother's final resting place.

Her third son, Glee, named Gladstone, realized his mother was especially sad on that day. He stopped playing ball with his just older brother named Leroy, called Roy, to comfort his mother. As Glee approached her, she looked up from her packing and said, "Why Glee you've brought me one of your sunny smiles! That is the reason I named you so, as you are joyous as the singing of a glee club! Come give me one of your special hugs."

As he gently hugged his mother, he laughed and said, "Roy just taught me how to swing that old stick like it was a silver dollar bat! Mother, I hope I grow up to be a baseball player and make lots of money just for you!" The tiny mother welcomed happiness in the simple pleasures of her sons playing a ball game. She thought about Glee's dream for the future. How so like him to be always thinking of her. She said a small prayer that all of her sons' dreams would all come true. After all, someone in this family deserved their dreams, she reflected. She told her boys to play a few minutes more, then to help finish the wagon packing for their westward journey.

She said, "Glee, Roy, you know if your Dad returns and this work is undone, he will be unhappy. So, boys five more minutes then make like you've been working all day."

Dutifully, the boys agreed to their gentle mother's request. After a few minutes playing as if the world series depended on them, they carefully put away their stick and ball. Although the stick was rough—hewn from a tree limb and the ball made from old twine dipped in glue, the two brothers love their homemade toys. Their six-month old baby sister Fairy Vivian sat in her crib and clapped her hands as her brothers ran around the bases of trees and rocks.

When the boys' tall rangy father returned from some errand, he found the two brothers, Roy and Glee hard at work while the younger boy named Joseph called Joe, drinking water from a pail by using a dipper. Vernie was busily helping her mother Rosa sort through quilts; they would need in New Mexico as the nighttime there was called as blanket nights for good reason. Fairy Vivian happily played with her toes and watched butterflies flying through the summer skies. The father, Lawrence, could not be gruff with his sons and one daughter appearing to do his bidding to complete all assigned tasks, while the baby seemed contented having nothing to cause crying. With each trip, the boys carried far heavier loads than their young bodies could bear. Vernie lifted even more quilts into the wagon, stopping only to tickle Fairy Vivian's toes as she passed by her baby sister's crib.

Their father found only finished chores. He looked for hints of misbehavior. Sternly he told his family they should eat, get on the wagon, and go west. He said, "I will make twenty miles a day before we stop to grease the axles. Even then, it will take us 12 or 13 days to get to Berlin, OK then another 10 or 11 days to Quay. This trip will not be like the Oklahoma failures of wild women roving our claim markers and a baby coming way too early yet causing delays."

Roy groaned, thinking, "Those poor animals won't survive the trip! He kept his thoughts to himself knowing his father never considered animals to be more than a tool to accomplish a job.

Glee whispered to Roy, "Golly, I'll get behind the wagon, way behind so if I see any wild fruit, I can gather it for Mother.

Roy quieted Glee by whispering, "You stay up with us and keep your eyes open for the wild fruit. Just tell me when you see any. It would break Mother's heart if you got lost."

After the hurriedly eaten meal, the last of the family's possessions were loaded onto the wagon. Their father lifted Joe with his tin cup of milk onto the wagon seat. Then he lifted the crib filled with Fairy Vivian into the wagon behind Joe. He growled to Glee and Roy to walk with the cow, two hogs, and three dogs in a fast march. He told the two brothers he would be driving the horses hard to make the twenty miles. He frowned at Vernie brushing her hair, making it ready for a new ribbon lying on Rosa's lap. He just knew the ribbon would be blowing in the wind shortly and possibly spooking one of the animals. He thought such things a waste as he absent-mindedly rubbed at the pain stabbing his stomach. He did not realize he was suffering from stomach ulcers.

It all seemed as final to their petite mother as she held back the tears and calmed her upset stomach, while closing the door of their Kansas home. She knew it was time to go forward to the promised rich soil and free land in New Mexico. She held a tiny hope thinking . . . "Just maybe Lawrence will be happy with a piece of his own railroad granted land."

The long grueling day wore into night. As a cloudy dusk turned darkly to a night without stars or moon, the father ordered his family to stop. He was angry at having traveled only seventeen miles because a wagon wheel fell off. The repairs used precious travel time. To ease his father's unkind words, Glee gave his mother the wild plums he had found while waiting for wagon wheel repairs. He told her how he found the plums and carefully gathered them into the milk pail. He asked if he could help her prepare plum pudding.

The tiny mother hugged her son saying, "Yes, and your help will be welcome since it is hard to see in the ever darkening night." After a supper of soup hastily warmed over a campfire and delightfully warm plum pudding wafting it cinnamon aroma, the father told his family 23 miles would be traveled the next day to make up for lost miles of today. Roy seethed with wild anger and glared at his father's latest command. Roy found the old burlap bag he had stowed in the wagon. He used the bag to rub down the horses, paying special attention to their legs and hooves. He found Brownie had a loose horseshoe and a swollen sore on his fetlock. Glee helped him find the liniment for old Brownie who nibbled both boys hair in appreciation of their care. Their father massaging his stomach yelled at them to get into their bedrolls. Roy could endure no harsh remarks.

He said, "Sir, Dad, I'm tending the horses so we can make 23 or more miles tomorrow. Brownie HAD a loose shoe!"

The father, moving his left hand slowly across his midriff mumbled, "Too much tending spoils the old nags."

With that Roy, hurried his brothers into their bedrolls, while their sweet mother bid them a good rest with a gently touch of her tiny hand.

Darkly early the next morning, the tall lanky father noisily prepared the wagon tongue and horses. He harshly told his Rosa to "Get all the day sleepers out of their bed rolls."

The youngest boy, Joe cried at awakening so abruptly early. Joe rubbing his tiny closed fist in his eyes while asking for milk. Baby Fairy Vivian happily nursed her mother's milk.

Roy said, 'Mother, I'll get the cow to give us milk, you have enough to do."

With that, Roy turned quickly on his heel to avoid giving his father a what for look, which could result in cuffing remarks. Gently Roy took his little brother's hand and told him Mama Cow would gladly give her milk to him. Little Joe sat wide-eyed, eagerly watching Roy milk the warm frothy liquid into the bucket. After the pail was nearly full, Roy kindly helped his small brother drink the warm milk from the edge of the pail. Then he took the pail of milk to his mother. She smiled sweetly at her sons in appreciation of their cooperation.

The day's early start did not set well with Glee who was watching the breakfast cook over the campfire while loading the wagon. The rocks were cold and sharp to his bare feet. The campfire was unsteady due to the rising west wind. Even Little Joe fretted at helping his mother get the tin plates and cups from the wooden box. He usually enjoyed the pinging noise of the tin dishes, as soon he could have more milk. Even Vernie was not singing one of her little songs and she had not brushed her hair, to make it ready for one of her prized ribbons.

After the breakfast of Dutch oven biscuits, left over supper soup, and the remainder of the plum pudding all washed down with the still warm milk from Momma Cow, the father began barking his orders to his family. He told Roy to harness the horses to the wagon without brushing them.

He said, "Dang horses need a slap upside their heads to wake them up and show who is boss around here! Do not be giving them any feed either. They'll pull faster for me."

Roy meekly replied while gritting his teeth, "Sir, uh I got up extra early to tend the livestock. The horses have a feedbag I made so they could be in harness and eat at the same time we were eating. Sir, if that meets with your satisfaction."

Vernie and Little Joe flinched in fright at their father roaring about with his hand on his abdomen. Baby Fairy Vivian began crying. "That boy will ruin those gall darned critters, why they are just, just tools! "Sputtered the father. Mid-afternoon of the fifth day, the family came upon the raging rolling Canadian River as it boiled through the flat lands of western Oklahoma. In pure red anger, the father threw down his hat and cussed out the barrier to his travel. He demanded his family unload the wagon, saying he would drive it and the cow across the raging waters. If he made it, then the family could cross the rolling water on the horses.

Quick thinking Roy said, "Sir, if we leave the wagon loaded it will counter balance the river's forces. If you calculate . . ."

"Dang, boy your thinking is not doing!" . . . the father's roaring voice trailed into" . . . but you are right; the weight would hold the wagon steady. You stay here on the bank with your mother, brothers and sisters while I cross the dang nasty river."

The wee mother could bear no more; tears, silent tears flowed like two tiny rivers from her eyes down her high Huguenot cheek bones. She had lost too much and now could lose more to a craze driven, in a hurry to get to New Mexico, husband. Just what would she do if he lost the wagon and drowned in the rolling waters? How would she manage to save the remnants of her family? Just then, Little Joe began to whimper.

Glee found the remains of the morning milk in a fruit jar among the things cast off the wagon. Little Joe drank from the fruit jar and smiled. He began to play with small white rocks he found on the river's edge, as his mother turned her back to the angry river. She was unable to face the impending peril. Her family was so precious to her.

When the father returned to his family, he was leading the trembling aging horse called Brownie. Roy ran to his father with a look of deep pity in his eyes. His father said,

"Here, this old wind bag of bones made it. Get your Mother and Fairy Vivian on him with you and ride across the river."

With that demand barely out of his mouth, he scooped up Little Joe and roughly grabbed Glee by the arm. Little Joe wailed to ride with his mother. The wild ride across the river upset his stomach so much so that the warm now soured milk came upwards out of his mouth and down his father's back. The driven man did not notice the warm sour smell trailing behind him. He was too intent on getting his sons across the river on the younger of the two wagon horses. Glee having righted himself in front of his father could smell the terrible soured milk. He knew what Little Joe had done. Glee covered his mouth to stifle a giggle. If his raging father heard him laughing while crossing the boiling river, Glee was unsure of what would happen! Nevertheless, he knew Roy would enjoy knowing what their baby brother had done to the backside of their father! It would give much joy in the bedroll that night! Glee concentrated on remembering the facts so he could tell the story again to his eldest brother Leck when they reached the soddy house in Quay near Walker Mountain.

Suddenly Glee looked up and there were Mother, Fairy Vivian, and Roy! How did they get there ahead of them? In amazement he asked, "How did you do that?"

Roy calmly said, "I just gave Brownie his head and he found the narrow part of the river to cross. He gave Mother a rocking chair smooth ride and Fairy Vivian fell asleep." Their mother nodded in agreement and grinned at having her skirts remain dry due to her son's quick thinking.

Then she smelled her sour husband and laughed aloud at what her baby boy Joe had done in a moment of distress. She needed this release from pent up emotions of nearly losing her family. She took her little crying son and cuddled him.

The tall rangy father never understood his wife's laughter. She could laugh at things so unfunny. He thought it must be one of those woman things. He decided to keep his distance from her for the next few days.

To regain authority, the father yelled for Roy. He said, "Since you are so smart about the goll-dang river, you and your bag of bones of a horse can go get the stuff we left on the other side!"

Roy replied, "Yes, sir! Then under his breath, he said. "With pleasure." After several trips, all the family belongings were back in the wagon. The last item Roy pulled out of his shirt was the fruit jar of milk. Little Joe squealed with delight at the sight of the milk.

As his mother held the fruit jar to Little Joe's lips, she asked, "Roy, How did you cool this milk, son?"

He grinned saying, "Mother, I put a rope around it and drug it through the cool river."

The Mother just shook her head as her son's smart thinking. She knew in her heart he would do something good as a man for children.

Once again, the Father was angry over the lost miles and quickly fleeting time. He mercilessly drove the family until the moon was high in the western sky. All the while he kept his hand on his aching stomach. The family made a quick stop in Berlin, Oklahoma for Rosa to say a brief prayer over her mother's grave.

By chance, her father, Peter Klopfenstein was there and gave her a brief hug. He knew his daughter and family must move on. He handed Rosa a packet wrapped in satin. He said in broken English heavily accented by his Alsace Loraine voice, "Rosa, dear one, this is your Mother Sarah Jane's sewing reading glasses. The satin is from her wedding dress. She knew you loved her glasses. May they bring you comfort. You both are so alike." Then he hugged her again saying, "When you come back, please stop for a rest and a talk. You will come again."

Roy helped his mother into the wagon. He checked on the animals, then climbed into the wagon to give his mother a hug. She was caressing her mother's glasses. Roy was amazed at the reading glasses delicate shape. He told his mother how beautifully they sparkled in the moon light.

She said, "Son, since you appreciate their beauty, I will write in my Bible, that you are to have these reading glasses when my time on earth is finished."

Roy hugged his mother and said, "That won't be for a long, long time; but I will always cherish those glasses for I remember my Grandmother Sarah Jane was pretty and loved all of us. She made those quilts like painted pictures for all of her children just like the one you have packed in the hope chest for Vernie."

By dawn, the family had entered the badlands of Texas. Although they heard bandits and wild ones roamed the cap rock of far north Texas; they wanted to a stop for a rest and a meal. The father said, "No campfire, it will attract bad men for miles in this flat land. Just milk the cow and we will drink milk for a meal. That is, if you don't feed it all to Little Joe!"

While Roy was rubbing down Brownie with the burlap bag, he noticed the horse was heaving. Suddenly Brownie fell down. He neighed a pitiful sound, and stopped breathing. Roy could accept no more. His hard driving father had killed his horse! He ran to tell his father a thing or two. After showing Brownie to his father, Roy wished he could just run away.

His father said, "Good riddance! I will just hitch the cow to the wagon and we will be on our way to Quay. Guess ol' horse will be good coyote food tomorrow."

Roy explained to his Mother, brothers and sisters about Brownie's demise. He said, "Mother, the cow will quit giving milk, having to pull the wagon. We had better milk her again tonight and tomorrow. We can make butter and buttermilk to carry us into New Mexico." His Mother silently agreed with a nod of her head. She chased black thoughts from her mind by praying and mulling over what she hoped Leck had accomplished in with the Southern Pacific Railroad in Tucumcari, New Mexico.

Vernie took all her beloved hair ribbons and wrapped them in oiled paper. She thought better to save them in case we have more bad luck. Thereafter she wore an aged black string to tie her long blonde hair away from her face. She dreamed that she would one day wear colorful ribbons while being with her New Mexico cousins. She recited Fairy's poem, repeatedly. Lost in daydreams, she wished she could write poems.

Roy jarring her from her musings saying,
"Here is a ditty,
For my sister so pretty,
In Quay, you'll find a kitty.
With Meowing so witty."

"Oh, Roy!" she said. "It is unfair you can just roll the poems off your tongue while I struggle to memorize them. I must hurry to find a paper bag to write what you said before, I forget it all."

Roy gave her a hug and said, "If you forget, just ask and I will repeat it." Then jumped off the wagon to check animals' their oat bags . . .

Before dawn fully arrived, the father was yelling to move onward. Glee said he would milk Momma Cow while Roy harnessed the cow and horse to the wagon. Glee was doubtful the two would pull together. The dapple-gray belonging to his father was unpredictable, headstrong and an Appaloosa to make matters even worse. The gray horse named simply Horse and matched its headstrong master in stubbornness. After several false starts, the family was once again on their way. Late in the afternoon, the family was weary with the dry heat and keeping their eyes open for the deadly rattlesnakes. Horse had tried to break harness more than once after seeing a coiled rattling mass of trouble. The little mother was gravely concerned for her sons having to walk barefoot among the deadly snakes. She promised herself that never again would any of her children be barefoot. She would find a way to put shoes on their feet.

Glee said, "Look, Roy that has to be watermelons over there! All green and sweetly red inside! I am going for them!"

Roy grabbed his arm saying, "Now Glee, those don't seem big enough for watermelons. Hold on. Let us think about this for a bit. We cannot go running off and upsetting Mother."

There was no persuading Glee to abandon any possible fruit. He took off in a hard run for the melon patch. Suddenly, he yelled to the top of his lungs. "Oh, no there are huge Texas size stickers here! Goat heads you call them. Help, Help, And Help Me! Quick come and get me, Roy!" screamed Glee.

"Hold on! Hold on!" yelled Roy. He scrambled out of the wagon, dumping Vernie's ribbons and scattering her doll things all about. He was thinking what I could do now. Spying the hoe, he grabbed the hoe, bumping Fairy Vivian's crib. Then he whispered to Vernie and Mother. Do not worry. I will get him back from the stickers! "Roy ran to the edge of the thorns then began to use the hoe to sweep the thorny mass away from his own bare toes. All the while thinking, if a snake rears up, I'll chop chop his head off.

Roy reaching Glee, he asked, "How did you get this far without feeling the stickers?"

Glee grinned and replied, "Well, I ran so fast that the thorns did not stick me until this far into them. Now that you have a hoe, let's check the melons."

Roy started laughing and saying, "You silly willy these are citrons. They are so sour you will pucker all the all the way to Quay! Besides they aren't even ripe."

Glee sputtered, "But Mother could cook them into something!"

Roy laughed saying, "No, she doesn't have any sugar. But she can have some honey." Hearing a noise, Roy spotted bees buzzing into the hole of a tall but dead nearby cactus. "Come on my melon chasing brother; roll those citrons down the sticker free path I just hoed." said Roy.

The brothers followed the bees to the cactus. Roy used the hoe to break off a part of the cactus. The boys found the sweetest honeycombs. After having their fill, they carried the honey and rolled citrons to their mother.

She smiled at her smart boys. She said, "We will make a citron honey pudding tonight. Thank you, boys for finding the honey to sweeten things. You know honey is your father's favorite thing to eat. It eases his stomach pains."

That night at the western edge of Texas border near the eastern boundary of New Mexico, the family enjoyed their sweet treats with a bit of milk from Momma Cow. Even Fairy Vivian had given up crying about the discomforts of the hard trail ride. Their father said tomorrow would see them in New Mexico. The honey must have mellowed the father as he let the next morning's early rim of the sun awaken his family. They and the animals were grateful for the much-needed rest.

As the family entered the edge of Quay County, New Mexico Walker Mountain loomed in the foreground. Somewhere near the village of Tucumcari, the little Mother heard her eldest son Leck running and yelling, "Mother, Mother, Mother!"

Her heart soared having all her boys and girls together. She was thankful for the rising joy in her heart. She had not felt such happiness for a long while, she though as she lovingly stroked her Mother's satin covered eyeglasses case deep in her pocket.

Roy hugged his older brother and said "Glee and I have a lot to tell you!" Little Joe toddled up to his adored oldest brother and giggled. He pointed to his father's back still stained from little Joe's upset stomach caused by the wild river crossing. Leck just rolled his eyes knowing the tales would come later.

Leck said, "Sir, I tried to claim the land but they, er some tobacco chewing six gun toting women said I was too young for what they had in mind. It reminded me of your wild women encounter in Oklahoma. If we go now, we can be there in an hour and you can do the official claiming. Mother, it is special, I have a surprise."

The anxious father said, "Let's be off!"

Leck quietly said, "Come Roy and Glee, I have an extra horse. He is like Brownie." The brothers quickly jumped onto the back of a large sorrel with one white ear. Leck told Roy, "He has not been named, thought I would let you do that. So I did not see Ol' Brownie. Guess he was driven too hard."

Roy just nodded with a small tear in the corner of his left eye. Roy said, "Leck, you have been here only about six months or so. How did you earn enough for two fine horses and all that money?"

Leck replied, "Well, I met Mr. Widner at the blacksmith shop. He was having a terrible time with three of his water wells and the windmills. I offered to take a looksee for meals and a ride to his place. He took me up on the offer and I stayed on as hired help. He paid me in horses, feed, and a warm hayloft for sleeping, and his wife cooks real swell. Then he had a sow in real trouble trying to have piglets. I saved them all. Momma Sow and her 18 squealing pigs. Come weaning time, I get two of the piglets. What I make with the Southern Pacific railroad, I have made out just fine. What we fellows did with that spring fed water well we found for the Southern Pacific Railroad turned out grand. Those railroad guys; they set me up real good in the money department. That railroad water well will likely make it over a hundred years."

Roy grinned saying, "You always did know what to do with water wells and windmills! Mother will be so happy when you give her that money."

When the older boys and the family wagon arrived at the staked vast amount of land near Walker Mountain, their Mother got out of the wagon without assistance. She was in awe at the view before her. It was the most beautiful mountain she had ever seen.

Leck said, "Mother, I knew you would like this spot. We, Walker Bunch here, even named it Walker Mountain. We got a bunch of Walker Cousins here. I am too young to claim the land . . . oh here is Mr. Klopfenstein. He said he is your cousin. He got me away from those, those not so lady like women. He held the land until you and Dad could arrive. He remembers what happened in Oklahoma with the wild women making a woman only town. Mother, while he talks with Dad, come over here to see this view."

With all her sons, Vernie, and Fairy Vivian, surrounding the tiny Mother, she hummed a sweet tune. She was smiling at Leck trying to talk so much like one of the Walker Circle Letters, which had to be read over and over again. The brothers looked at each other and grinned, happily that their sweet Mother was again singing.

Leck scratched his head and said, "And that sod house backed into a cave over by the running brook, it is yours, Mother. I did it with the help of some Wyandot Indian friends, who may be kin to the Klopfenstein. I hope you like it. While it is, only a dugout house with dirt floor, the Wyandots wove cactus fibers with mesquite tree leaves to cover the floors. It is not yet finished and rains are coming. So we will be sheltering in another cave at the base of Walker Mountain for a while. I thought you and the girls could bed in the wagon after we back it into the cave. One of our cousins, Lawrence Ezra named after Dad, has carved his initials LEW in that cave."

"Say," said Roy, "Those are my initials too! I want to spend some time with that fine cousin! Wonder if he likes trains as much as you do, Leck?"

Oh yes, Mother here is money now don't you give any of it to Dad. It is for you when you need things. Out here you will need things." said Leck.

Their Mother with a happy face said, "Oh, Leck now all of my boys can have shoes. We will get them when we go into Grady or Quay. I suspect Roy will be eyeing boots which he talks about in his sleep. Also

Vernie needs a sturdier pair of shoes to deal with this cactus. And Fairy Vivian is out growing her clothes. I am so happy to have us all together because that is what it means to be a family. I need more talking time with you, Leck. I have never heard you talk so much like those Walker Circle Letters we send around to kinfolks."

While the family was checking out the dugout house, Fairy Pamelia saw Vernie Pamelia. She came riding up on her pony. She said, 'You must be my Kansas cousin with the same middle name as me. I am so happy to meet you."

As Vernie placed some hair ribbons in Fairy Pamelia's hand, she said,

"True Contentment means: Four walls can hold contentment
                                  Dear home where love and peace abide;
                                  Containing life's richest treasures
                                  Wherever we go, or what betide."

Then she giggled knowing cousins good times would be happening.

Fairy Pamelia said, "OH my, you know my poem. I have more poetry that we can share just for the fun of them.

Under the Firefly Moon

One still hot mid-June day in Sedan, Kansas, the elderly grandmother leaned on the doorframe for support. The sight unfolding before her eight decades of eyes tugged at her heart. Two tiny girls, ninety days apart in age, danced along a stone wall separating their grandparent's garden from a neighbor's yard. The girls thought to be the last of nine granddaughters and one grandson. The five-year-old girls sang their version of a song known to all children. As they held hands, pure angelic voices rang out, "Say, say, O playmate, come out and play with me. And bring your dollies three. Climb my pecan tree. Shout in my rain barrel. Slide down the cellar door. And we'll be jolly sister cousins. Forevermore, more. Say O say playmate I can't play with you. My dolly's got the flu Bo Hoo hoo. Ain't got no rain barrel; Texas is dry. Got a cellar door for when tornadoes hit and we will be sister cousins forevermore, more . . ."

One granddaughter lived in California. Her shy quiet nature was most enduring. She always had a good thing to say to everyone. She loved animals of all kinds. She had a very gentle spirit. She wanted to spend time with her older sister Alvena who always played games with her. Sometimes she read about farm animals, which made her smile. The other granddaughter lived in Texas. She was never still a moment. She was Tornado a nickname given by Alvena who thought she had two little sisters to watch over. Tornado's perpetual motion often marked by sign language tumbling off her fingers so her beloved deaf Mother would know what was happening. The girls' distant homes caused the grandmother to hold dear in her heart every moment she had with them. She pondered what lasting gifts she could bestow upon these cherished girls.

The grandmother's second son of five sons and father of the Texas Tornado asked, "Mother, why are you smiling through tear glistened eyes?", as he hugged her.

The tiny mother said, "Look and listen son, to those girls. Sharron and Daisy are like Vernie and Fairy, your sisters we lost long ago to illnesses."

As the high voices drifted through the screen door, "Oh no my dolly has the flu and I cannot slide down your cellar door. I cannot yell in your rain barrel, I cannot climb your pecan tree, boo hoo hoo!"

Roy gently hugged his aging and shrinking mother, as he said, "It is only a song. They always sing it. Listen to how they change the words around to fit them. Especially when they want Nat and me to think they are playing nicely; not dirtying the dresses which Jenny and Christine made for them."

Grandmother Rosa said, "Son, it is not the song so much as it is . . . they look and play like your sisters Vernie and Fairy did out in New Mexico, so very long ago. You recall when we went in search of land to make a homestead. Your older brother Leck went ahead of us to work on the railroad. And on the trail, you and your brother Glee found those citrons thinking they were melons."

Roy replied, "You are right, Mother. It is amazing how you remember my sisters so well. They have been gone nearly four decades. And as for my brothers, well, Ma'am some things are best left on the trails of life."

"Son, a mother never forgets lost children. Somehow, though, I've been given a gift in these granddaughters. They are so like your sisters. Did you know Vernie sang that song to Fairy? These girls are filling the hole in my heart left by the loss of your three sisters. I just wish the baby's grave could be found in Oklahoma Territory."

"So, Mother when Dad calls them Vernie and Fairy, you don't mind? You don't see Dad as being sick and lost in time?" asked Roy.

"That is correct, son. Those girls are near replicas of the real thing. And someday they will help my heart find Clisty Jane the dear baby lost during the Indian Territory Land runs of 1892." She replied.

"Well, I'll be . . ." exclaimed Roy not finishing his thoughts. "Mother, I need to drive Nat to the car repair garage. Glee agreed to look at the old Plymouth that he wants to use to pull a trailer house all the way to California.," explained Roy. He shared that Glee, as supervisor, at the Sedan Ford Motor Company, had agreed to check their youngest brother is ailing car. Then he said, "Christine and Jenny are preparing our supper and they ask that you watch the girls so they cook something real tasty. Mother, you know how Christine wants to keep a close eye on them since she cannot hear. Are you sure those girls won't tire you out?"

She replied, "Son what tires me is not having those little girls around to make me smile. You know they are so alike yet so different. Everyone thinks Sharron is never part of the pranks. Which are always blamed on Daisy. Well, I have seen Sharron make plans to pull a funny trick. Son, it will be a joy to see what they get into this time. You know I will watch them carefully while Christine and Jenny fry those chickens as only they can do. See that large apricot cobbler they made for the family supper. It will be such fun to have the house with all the joy and laughter."

"Thank you Mother, It means a lot to Christine for you to watch those girls. Since she cannot hear, she needs to know trustworthy eyes are on them. She and Jenny do not want them straying too far from the house. They also do not want them wandering downtown toward that ice cream shop where those tykes can get a cone just by smiling at Mr. Widner.," explained Roy.

"Yes, son, I know the story of when Nat and Jenny stayed with you and Christine for awhile in Texas. Those girls started a big fire so you and Nat could cook mountain oysters and frog legs. I also know Jenny and Christine are good mothers. They have their daughters' best interest in mind. That's all I've got to say about watching those girls!" exclaimed the tiny grandmother.

"Yes, Yes, Mother, Nat and I will pay dearly into eternity for letting those girls start the camp fire and for allowing them to eat those mountain oysters. To this day, Nat and I can hear Christine saying in her deaf voice, 'Shame on you men for feeding those girls bull parts. How can Jenny and I teach them to be ladies! It will be your fault if they turn into Wild Walker Women!' Mother, Jenny still prays every night about that fire and it has been over a year since they were in Texas." Roy explained sheepishly.

"Never the less," replied the grandmother, "You should have asked Jenny and Christine if the girls could eat . . . Uh . . . wild game."

Just then, the tiny girls ran onto the screened porch saying, "Grandfather is awake. We head him through his window. Then off they scurried to find their elderly frail grandfather sitting on the side of his bed. When he saw them, he said, "Vernie and Fairy come tell me a story. I do so miss hearing a good story. I have slept too long and too hard. Your story will help me wake up to bright day."

The girls said, "Granddad, we're Sharron and Daisy. We're playmates and cousins. We have been singing songs and walking the stone wall beside your house."

Grandfather asked, "Why are you moving your hands?"

"'Cause drawled Daisy, If Mother walks in, she'll know what we are saying. You remember, Mother can't hear."

"Oh yes, Roy's wife, the deaf red haired one who makes fried chicken. Say do I smell frying chicken?" the Grandfather rambled.

"Yes, sir answered Sharron. "Yes and Grandmother had to kill three of her best chickens because the supper table will be full of family tonight. And Daisy pitched a Texas Tornado fit!"

"Why did she do that?" asked the Grandfather.

"Well, Sharron slowly answered, "Grandmother started chopping the chicken necks. But Daisy with her hands flying all over ran squalling to Aunt Christine."

Grandfather asked, "What happened then?"

Sharron took a deep breath and said, "Aunt Christine ran out to the chicken stump and twisted the chickens necks and the chickens flipped flopped with no heads across the yard!"

"Oh, those Texans are real different, Vernie." said Grandfather.

"Yeah, I saw Aunt Christine twist chickens necks lots and lots when we were in Texas. Boy, it kinda scares me." Sharron softly replied.

Daisy said, "Oh, Granddad, hatchets are so mean. Let's go get some buttermilk."

Sharron cried aloud, "EEEEEEEUUUWEEE, not, that old sour milk!"

Grandfather laughed and said, "It is good, Vernie come try some." Both girls helped their frail grandfather walk to the kitchen. He patted each one on their head.

After she helped him to his chair, Daisy brought three glasses filled with creamy white liquid. She giggled and said, "Sharron, here's your BUTTERmilk. Yours is different."

As Sharron made a scowling face, she tasted her glass of creamy cold liquid. Then, she smiled and said, "I just don't believe you! You poured the cream just for me."

"And that is not all sister-cousin, looky, I snitched three apricot cookies. I said to Aunt Jenny 'Granddad needs them 'cuz he is tired from all that sleep." giggled Daisy.

Sharron whispered, "You are so sneaky. I love you for getting my favorite cookie. Let's go play jacks after we finish our cookies and milk. Granddad can sit in the rocker and watch. He likes to think he is taking care of us."

Grandfather dreamily looked at the energetic happy girls. He said, "Vernie, Fairy that chicken your Mother is cooking smells good. I hope there is enough for you two girls."

Sharron said, "Oh Granddad that is Aunt Christine cooking the chicken and my Mother is fixing the potatoes. There always is more than enough food when Mother and Aunt Christine are in the kitchen. Besides you know the other aunts will bring their stuff."

Just then, the tiny Grandmother came to the table. She said, "Lawrence, I am not cooking today. Christine and Jenny are making dinner so we can enjoy our youngest granddaughters. Remember, your sons, Roy and Nat came for a visit? They brought their daughters. You know Sharron was born on Roy's birthday and Nat is still grumbling because Daisy was not born on his birthday."

Grandfather's fading memory could not grasp and retain things told to him. It seemed these were his daughters, but he thought somewhere in time he had lost his girls. As for Roy and Nat, he had told them to plow the south ten acres so the corn planting could begin. He was so sure but could not remember where or how anymore. If only he could arrange his thoughts. It all seemed so jumbled and tumbled with plowing, three funerals and . . . when the ringing telephone dispelled all of his thoughts.

Daisy, never wanting to miss an opportunity to talk, ran to answer the telephone. After the first Howdy, she drawled, "Weeelll, hello Big Brother Bud!" She giggled then asked, "What secret, can you tell me? Really, wowow, for sure, Granddad will love it. Sure, we have tons of ice . . . uh . . . I will tell you why later we have lots of ice. Me, not me I would not turn the ice card to fifty pounds so the ice man brought too much ice yesterday. Yes. I'll tell Grandmother. By Y'All" she said as she hung up the telephone on wall. She was careful to avoid the crank handle as that would get the operator on the line and she did not tolerate any kids on the phone party line. The operator always said, 'Number please and this house is making many calls today.'

She ran to her Mother who was turning the chicken frying in a large black cast iron skillet. She signed without using her voice, "Mother, a secret, a surprise. Bud's coming after supper. He's coming with Aunt Hallie. He is bringing a freezer so we can make ice cream for Granddad. You tell Dad we really do need all that ice after all. Oh, goody!"

Daisy ran with joy to her Grandmother and Sharron. She sang, "It is a tisket it is a tasket I've got a great big secret in my egg basket. Grandmother, let's check for eggs in the hen house. We can take the yellow secret basket I like the yellow one best of all your baskets."

Grandmother smiled and kissed her granddaughters, she said, "Okay, let's go. They walked through the fragrant kitchen, onto the screened back porch; pass the vegetable garden to the hen house. Hens were softly clucking and settling upon their nests, while the one rooster pranced around the floor. He was ready to crow but there was no rising sun or freshly laid eggs to crow about.

Sharron said, "Me, too, I want to see the hens and eggs. But most of all I want to hear the secret." As the trio walked into the hen yard, Sharron demanded, "What is the secret?"

Daisy answered, "What secret?" with a gleam in her eyes and a giggle escaping her lips . . . "Come on Sister Cousin, let's get the eggs." As the girls entered the chicken coop, Daisy said, "I got the secret and I am gonna tell Sharron. Our Big Brother Bud is coming with Aunt

Hallie. I love him so much—he is handsome and he always has a book about trains. He has three sisters, Rose Mary, Janice, and Jeanne. They are all grown up. Well except Janice. She is in high school and she is really lots of fun."

Sharron said, "He is our cousin, silly. I just don't believe you. You always have secrets and I never have any."

"He can be our Big Brother, if we want. Where else are we gonna get a brother? Besides, he's got all sisters and he knows how to read to us—oooh—I just love his books!" replied Daisy.

Sharron said, "Oh, oh, he did climb the apricot tree just for me. When we had that family picnic, he was so nice to us. Maybe . . . ,"

Daisy interrupted with, "Oh, I almost forgot—he is bringing the ice cream freezer to make ice cream to go on top of the apricot cobbler that Aunt Jenny made. Yummy to our tummy!"

Grandmother held the egg basket as her granddaughters gathered eggs from the clucking hens. On fat Rhode Island Red hen tried to peck Sharron's hand as she slid it under its feathers.

Daisy shouted, "Mother will wring your neck and make you into a roasted hen if you hurt Sharron!" With that commotion, the fat old hen waddled away from her nest holding four large eggs. The rooster looked cross eyed at the commotion and gave out half of a crow.

Sharon asked, "You are not afraid of anything are you? You just go around telling chickens to move on over!"

"I'm no 'fraidy cat of fat hens. They are just baked chicken and dressing walking around on legs." giggled Daisy.

Grandmother said, "Dears, I love your secret. You girls are such fun with your harmless pranks. You are so like each of your Dads in fun making. Yet, you have your Mothers to keep you in line. Let's get these eggs back to the kitchen. Then you girls can take Granddad to the front porch. He likes to watch the cars going up and down the street. Sometimes folks stop to chat with him and that makes him smile."

Sharron said, "He really likes to watch us play jacks and jump rope. We'll do that just for him. Besides, we have a new jacks game. Pigs in the fence."

Daisy wrinkled up her nose and exclaimed, "Phew, stinko, I don't like pigs. You know we have a fat old wobbly dumb sow. It is my job to feed her. She is so dumb she thinks I'll eat her slop. She runs at me. I wish dad would make her into ham and bacon!"

Grandmother shockingly said, "Why, Honey, I thought you loved all animals!"

"No Ma'am er Yes Ma'am, just not hogs! Hogs are for Sharron to love." drawled Daisy. "Hogs are real dumb dumbs. They won't learn anything so I don't like 'em." Then she sauntered onto the porch imitating the waddle walk of a sow Grandmother tried to hide her smile as she thought, 'That one will tear through Texas like one of its tornadoes someday!' She said, "Girls, show me your shiny new jacks. Let's get Granddad settled in the rocker on the front porch. I really need you girls to help me watch him. But most of all he needs a smile today. He slept too long and too hard for a nap."

Daisy said, "Yes, Ma'am, we will. You know Grandmother; all he really needs is lots of love and a few giggles. Sharron and I will sing our Playmate Song 'cause he always laughs at that. We might tell him about all the barn cats."

Sharron said, "Yeah, and he calls us Vernie and Fairy . . . that's okay dokey, too. We can pretend to be his daughters, really they are our aunts gone to heaven. We wish we could know them but maybe they would make us wear those long dresses instead of these play suits."

"Granddad, we're finished gathering eggs, come to the front porch so we can play jacks, you can help us keep score. Sharron always takes extra turns with pigs in the pen, pigs in the fence, pigs in anything; 'cause she loves stinky hogs." said Daisy.

"I do not take extra pigs in the pen turns. Hogs don't stink. They are cute even when they jump in the mud and oink around.," replied Sharron.

"Weeelll," drawled Daisy, "Like when we jumped in the mud puddle after Aunt Jenny and Mother made us dresses? You know the pink and yellow ones like the leftover material they gave Grandmother for her quilt box. We had to take a second bath and go to bed for a nap. That was your idea to pretend to be piglets and jump in the mud like pigs do. I got the blame for it! Besides they are stupid, they can't make up stories or read! They certainly don't wear dresses!"

"Girls! Now, be nice before your Mothers remember your pretending to be piglets in mud puddles and you have to go to bed again." said their Grandmother.

"That's it, Come on Granddad let's go to the front porch. I got the jaaaaacks, not Sharron." Drawled Daisy as the tottering elderly man slowly walked through the house to the front porch.

Grandmother said, "Lawrence, you sit here and watch these girls play their game. The iceman will be coming soon and I will have to tell him we don't need any more ice. And Lawrence, these girls should stay on the porch to be safe. I still do not trust cars going up and down the street; as they might jump the curb onto the sidewalk and harm our girls."

Sharron exclaimed, "Onesies are done, I did not drop any so I can play twosies now!" As she threw a handful of shiny jacks across the cool porch floor, she hummed the Playmate song to herself and thinking how much fun it is to play jacks.

"Great pigs feet, I'll just jump my rope that Dad made for me until you miss." replied Daisy.

"Don't say pig feet, oh drat you made me drop twosies, Overs, Overs!" shouted Sharron before her cousin could call Kings X. Grandfather smiled as the girls giggled.

"YAll always say 'Overs, Overs' to get another turn. Well, just take it. I'd rather jump rope. This reminds me of JoJo dog at home. He jumps when we feed him. I have to tell Alvena, 'cause he is really her dog. She got him as a pup when she lived with Dad. Do you know Alvena put JoJo in a big black old bag she found in the trash? I would never put any pup in a stinky like hogs black bag gotten out of the trash."

"Gosh, it's no fun winning a turn if you give up. I want you to make a joke of it. Oh, I might as well teach you the new Pigs in the Fence jacks game. Now, watch me. See, you hold this hand like a fence, bounce the ball once. While the ball is in the air, sweep one pig . . . er . . . jack in the fence. It is fun to do that is if you didn't jump so hard on the porch to make the pigs . . . er . . . jacks wiggle!" explained Sharron.

"Sharron, jacks are not pigs! Pigs don't wiggle like a pretty lady walking, pigs waddle like this." said Daisy as she bent her legs and wavered side to side across the porch.

"I just don't believe you!" shouted Sharron. "Granddad, please tell her pigs can too wiggle. The lady pigs do to wiggle when they walk!"

Just at that moment, the iceman stopped his ice truck at the curb. Daisy ran out to ask him questions. She asked, 'Sir, Mr. Iceman, tell my cousin and Granddad only pretty ladies walking wiggle while pigs waddle 'cause they just do." She pranced and wiggled up and down the sidewalk to show how a pretty lady wiggle is done.

The ice delivery man grinned at the tyke. He knew she was the Walker grandchild from Texas. Who having just the day before, turned the ice ordering card placed in the front screen door from its usual ten pound order to a whopping fifty pound order. He said, "Good afternoon, Mr. Walker, I see you are watching your granddaughters. How is the Texas Tornado doing today, sir? Has she melted all that fifty pounds of ice, yet? I'd like to sell you more ice but there is no room for it in your icebox."

Granddad slowly replied, "Why, these little girls are Vernie and Fairy, our daughters. They are playing right nice and I am having a pleasant time with them. As for the ice, you better ask Rosa, their mother. She is in charge of a big supper tonight. All the boys will be coming in from the farm real soon."

"Yes, sir." the iceman said as Grandmother appeared from behind the screen door.

Grandmother said, "We have enough ice for two days. But thank you for stopping by. I hear Daisy is asking you about a pig's waddle. Are you going to answer her question? She won't let you get away without some kind of answer."

"Well . . . uh . . . I don't have much pig experience except that is eating bacon or ham and such. I don't rightly know how they walk. As for ladies sashays, I er don't know anything about that sort of thing." said the iceman.

Daisy said, "See, he thinks pigs are better as bacon, Shaaarron!"

"Oh, I just don't believe you! You wiggle walked up the sidewalk! Granddad, tell her to be nice! That is so embarrassing." cried Sharron.

The iceman said, "Mr. & Mrs. Walker, I better be going to complete my rounds. I will see you in a couple of days. Little Walker girls, so long." As he made a hasty retreat to his truck to avoid any further questions about pig waddles or lady sashays while laughing at the girls antics behind his hand covering his mouth.

Grandmother said, "Lawrence, I need to check on some things in the kitchen. You just make sure these girls stay on the porch with their jacks and jump rope."

Daisy ran to hug her Grandfather. She replied, "Grandmother, I will tell him a story until Sharron misses again. We will be fine." When the Grandmother was out of hearing distance, Daisy began the story.

"Once upon a time there was a great fat pig and my Daddy said he would get me some ham. So Daddy got his shotgun that went BANG BANG . . ."

Sharron cried out loud with instant tears. "No! No! Not Uncle Roy's big old black gun!"

Granddad said, "Shush, girls, you'll have Mother out here. Then I can't do the hand walking. She forbids it! And you will miss all the fun of it"

Both girls looked at their Grandfather with wide-eyed surprise. At the same time they asked, "What is hand walking?"

Their Grandfather replied, "Girls, it is something all us Walker men can do. It is because we are Walkers." Suddenly, their Grandfather was upside down with his hands on the sidewalk. He was walking on his hands to the delight of his granddaughters. They clapped their hands with much joy. They laughed loudly.

As coins, a knife, pieces of string, a fish hook, and a pocket watch fell from his upside down pockets, Daisy said, "OOOOOHHH, Granddad, Sharron and I will pick up your things. We will hold them for you. We have nice big pockets on our playsuits."

He replied, "Good, I can think real well this way. Now you girls stay right behind me. I am going to walk the two block to town, turn right and take you both to the ice cream parlor. I want some ice cream right now. How about you girls?"

Sharron said, "But, Grandmother said . . ."

As Daisy interrupted her with, "All she said was 'Be nice'. We will be nice if we help Granddad with his things. Besides, he can't eat all that ice cream by himself. And what if he gets lost? We gotta go to help him. I want to watch him hand walk. It's great. Maybe we can learn how to do that too."

"Oh, okay, if you think that is being nice." Sharron meekly agreed. She thought some ice cream in a cone would be delicious and fun.

As the upside Grandfather hand walked and the girls slowly skipped their way behind him down the two blocks to Main Street. No cars or people passed them. The afternoon heat has most folks inside their homes either fanning themselves with the paper fans from the Methodist Church or they were drinking ice cold drinks and dozing with small naps. After the trio carefully turned the corner, their Grandfather said, "I better turn right side up so I can open the door to the ice cream parlor. You tykes might not be able to twist the old brass knob. Mr. Widner is very careful about that brass knob. You will like meeting him. He has some family off in Montana, no its Wyoming, er, well anyway, his son Don is visiting here this summer. I think he is courting Alvena. But don't tell your Grandmother. You know Grandmother would have out her Bible and a million questions for that poor kid."

Both girls hugged each other in wide-eyed amazement. Sharron whispered, "It's true. Loving Granddad made him remember stuff." They handed coins and other things dropped during the hand walking back to their Grandfather. He placed each item in its proper pocket. He patted each pocket to make sure the items were safe and secure.

He turned to Mr. Widner and said, "Good afternoon, sir. My granddaughters and I are hungry for some of your best ice cream. I suspect Sharron wants a dip of apricot and a dip of chocolate while Daisy would like a dip of Texas peach and a dip of Texas pecan. You know these are my last and youngest granddaughters. They have been playing jacks and jump rope. They have been singing that popular Playmate song and telling me stories. Right entertaining they both are."

The wide-eyed girls covered their open mouths as Mr. Widner said, "Sure, Mr. Walker, coming right up. And I suppose you will have you traditional vanilla. You must be feeling good lately to have walked these girls to my shop. How is Rosa doing?"

Sharron whispered to Daisy, "Again, I just don't believe you. All that love for Granddad made him remember who we really are. And the best of all he knows our favorite ice cream. He got you the Texas stuff 'cause all you talk about is how everything is bigger and better there. If you get bigger dips than I get, I am going to say, Overs, Overs!"

"Shush, Sharron. Overs is only for jaaacks, not ice cream cones.," drawled Daisy.

Daisy noticed a small table with some books in the corner of the ice cream shop. She asked, "Mr. Widner, is it alright if I read one of the books on the table?"

Mr. Widner replied, "Sure thing Little Texas. I like your drawl. I would like it better if you would read the books out loud. Do you start school early down there in Texas?"

Before he could finish his sentence, Sharron interrupted, "OOOOO Me too! I love it when she reads to me."

"Okey, dokey, after I eat my ice cream cone and all No sir I am not in school yet. My Mother and Dad taught me to read. Lots and lots of newspapers come to our house as my mother cannot hear but she read lots. Mostly Dad and I read about baseball and the funnies.," said Daisy.

After the last bit of ice cream was licked away, Sharron said, "Now we can go read the books. I hope you can read all of them."

"Oh, this will be Sharron's favorite, *Three Little Pigs*. I bet she squeals over this one!" exclaimed Daisy. "Once upon a time there were three brother pigs who . . . ," read Daisy. As she read on, the little ice cream shop began to fill with people wanting to cool off the Kansas summer heat. After placing their orders, they lingered to listen to the story being read by the tiny girl with a huge Texas drawl. They watched the other girl patiently holding several books to be read. She seemed most happy with the never-ending stories.

As the shop filled, Grandfather began to help Mr. Widner scoop the ice cream from the various large tubs. Both elderly men enjoyed the tasks. They joked around and gave a smile to each and everyone. When all customers were served, Mr. Widner looked in his cash register. He exclaimed, "Gosh, Mr. Walker, I have made more money today than any other day this summer! I wonder if it is the heat or the stories. That's it folks really like hearing the stories so they stayed longer then bought ice cream to take home. Mr. Walker, I sure do thank you for bringing those girls in and for helping me with all the customers."

The Grandfather smiled and replied, 'Oh think nothing of it. It feels good to be useful again. And those girls, well I had to find a way to keep them out of harms' way for a time. Rosa is busy in the kitchen you know. And when the house is filling up with family and their wives, it is best to have some time away from all those ladies."

While all seemed well, with the folks, enjoying their cold savory treats and listening to the stories partly being read and most being told from memory. The Walker family on Chautauqua Street was in distress. Roy, Nat and Glee returning from the Ford Motor Company, found all the women crying and praying. Roy was finally able to learn amid the sobbing that the little girls and their Grandfather were missing. Their Mothers and Grandmother had searched house, garage, hen house, neighbor's yards, houses, garages, the nearby park and even the vacant schoolyard.

As Jenny explained the details leading up to the search, Leck, the eldest Walker brother and his wife Edith drove up to the curb in front of the Walker home. Leck exclaimed, "Roy, its swell to see you again but not like this! I just heard over the two-way radio that Dad and the Little Ones are missing. It said Jenny had called the Sedan, Caney, and even Coffeyville police! What's happening?"

Roy removing his cowboy hat, scratched his head saying, "Well, I suspect they are fine but Nat and I will have to face the wrath of Jenny, Christine, and Mother until we locate the scamps. Got any ideas? Leck? Glee? Nat? There won't be a minute's peace or any supper on the table until we find the missing trio."

As the four brothers huddled together to discuss what should be done, Edith and Jenny went into the house to pray even more for the eldest and youngest missing family members Every Bible in the house was open to a favorite passage as it lay upon the dining room table.

Lois and Helen, daughters of Leck and Edith arrived at the Walker home. They explained their having been at the Methodist Church practicing for their special duet for Sunday's joint church services. Helen cried, "Oh, my we must find those little girls. They're so tiny and innocent! They cannot just disappear!"

To which Roy replied, "Now Helen, I wouldn't go far with the innocent bit, just yet! Let us find out why Dad is missing along with them. You know all three are just children, really."

And Nat added, "You just haven't seen some of the pranks Sharron and Daisy have pulled. That's it! They have pulled another fast one. I'll lay odds on it! Every time they pull a fast one, I get the blame for it. Then Jenny and Christine tear into me. You know we will have to go to church on Sundays and Wednesday nights forever!"

Glee looked up and said, "Why there is Jeanette and Jessie. They've been shopping for Connie and Larry. They have just come from Wichita. I expect they don't even know Dad and the girls are missing."

Jessie and Christine hugged each other. Christine told her tale of the missing girls and Granddad. Jessie assured her deaf but not so silent sister-in-law, that all would be well.

Jeanette pulled Connie and Larry even closer to her. She could not bear to think of her two little tykes as ever missing for even a moment. Glee hugged his daughter and grandchildren while saying, "Jeanette it won't happen to these little ones. Everything will work out. Why even Roy said, 'It's one of the girls' pranks' . . . it must be so. I just can't figure out how Dad is involved in their prank. He has been so unwell as of late."

Another car pulled up to the curb in front of the Walker home. The street was beginning to resemble a used car lot with so many vehicles parked on the street. This time it was Jeanne and Earl having come from Topeka for a special mechanical part available only in Sedan. Earl explained the International Harvester owner told them Jeanne's Granddad and two little girls, his youngest grandchildren, were missing. Jeanne having a soft place in her heart for children could not accept the news. She said she wanted to call her Dad, Joe the only Walker brother not at the house. Jeanne gave her Grandmother a hug and a kiss while saying, "Grandmother, they'll be found. I just need to call Dad. Maybe he and Bud will have an idea about Granddad and the girls He always has ideas how to find things that get lost around the house."

Grandmother explained Bud and Hallie were arriving any minute as they had called earlier. She shared how excited Sharron and Daisy were to know their "Big Brother" as they called their cousin Bud would be bringing his ice cream freezer. With that, Jeanne agreed to wait a few minutes before calling her Dad as he may have returned from the antique auction in time to drive down with Mother and Bud.

Daisyann Walker Palmer, PhD

Still another car parked on Chautauqua Street. The arrivals were Frank and Rose Mary with their first little one in their arms. Frank explained while at his parents' home he heard the news on the radio. Rose Mary interrupted with, "Somebody needs to do something quick! What if they have been kidnapped?" This set off another round of crying, sobbing, and praying.

Christine said, "I read your lips! Maybe they were taken." She turned to Roy and demanded he start a search party. Few understood the sign language but all knew her demands would not be ignored. Roy calmly held her hands and explained in sign language his view was that the girls had pulled a prank and would come rolling home like bad little pennies. Which he intended to shine up with a talk and the switch kept on top of a doorframe in his Mother's kitchen.

Yet another car parked some distance from the Walker home. It was Gene, Jeanette's husband. He said he had been practicing his guitar with a local band that would be raising funds for volunteer firefighters. He said the fire station emergency radio came on in the middle of their practice session of "Walking the Floor Over You." He commented how appropriate that song was as he could imagine a lot of floor walking happening at the Walker home. Gene being especially soft hearted toward his deaf aunt, gave her a warm hug and slowly spoke to her. He assured her all the missing family members would be found very soon. He said all the volunteer firefighters were going to search the entire town.

"We will find them. The firefighters' dog Cinder will help. You know Cinder can smell anything, even sweet little girls. And Aunt Christine, she is deaf like you, so you just be patient and wait on that Dalmatian. Let her smell something belonging to Granddad, as she knows him best of all. Then she can track them down." Christine ran quickly getting the blanket that Grandfather had used for his recent nap.

Gene asked Roy, "Did you bring your mandolin and violin? Later we'll make some good songs for all the folks when the girls and Granddad return. They will come back. I am sure."

Roy wiped his eyes and said, "I sure hope so." Then he looked up to see Alvena and some fine looking young man parking a fancy red car nearly a block away. Roy muttered, "Now, who does that young buck think he is holding my girl's hand? I suppose he's, he's . . ."

When Alvena saw her beloved uncle, she worked away her tightly held hand and ran to hug her uncle. She said, "Oh, Uncle Roy, I am so happy to see you but we heard Granddad and those girls. Oh I can't bear it, my sweet little sister Sharron is missing." Then Alvena's tears poured forth like a Kansas frog-strangling rainstorm. Roy comforted Alvena.

The young man having driven her to the Walker home nervously shuffled his feet and awkwardly held his hands behind his back. Roy, thinking to soothe Alvena, explained his theory of the girls having pulled a prank. Then Alvena instantly stopped crying and yelled, "That's it! That little Texas Tornado pride of your heart did it! She led sweet little Sharron and Granddad off someplace! You don't think so, but she did, she did."

"Now, now Alvena-girl." Roy hushed. "Don't go blaming her for sure until we find them. You know Dad might have just forgotten where he was. After all he has not been well."

To which Alvena replied, "All the more reason to suspect Daisy!"

Roy asked, "Say who is this . . . er . . . handsome young man?"

"Oh, Uncle Roy, I am ashamed. I forgot to . . . and er . . . uh . . . It was supposed to be so special but those naughty girls. They've ruined my special plans. You see this is Don . . . Don Widner. I or we were planning . . ."

Roy interrupted her with, "Gosh, another Don? That makes five or six you have dated. Alvena-girl you are gonna fool around until you end up marrying one of those Dons! Don't you like guys any other name? Now don't you start thinking marriage because you are way too young at seventeen to even think about marrying anyone?"

Alvena burst into tears again. Only this time she cried hot tears of rage as she blubbered, "Oh Uncle Roy, we were planning to ask you if we could get married next year. The day after you and Aunt Christine got married. June 26 would be a special day for us. We don't want to take your anniversary day but we want to be next to you. I've told Don all about you. Yes, even living in Texas with and Jo-Jo dog. I even told him the old black bag story. He knows all about it so don't go telling him stuff about me dragging the bag out of some lady's trash."

Her Uncle Roy grinned at the beautiful young woman standing before him and said, "Well, sure, next year, Alvena-girl. June 26 would be a fine marring day. In fact, it will always be a special day in the Walker family. So now, you have done it, gone and picked out a Don. Did you find a Big Old Black Bag to trap him or is that only for Texas pups? Bet he would not take to being stuffed in a hot black bag. Especially one taken out of stinky trash."

"Oh Uncle Roy, hush with telling tales on me!" responded Alvena.

"Have you asked your Dad, yet? He is in the house getting a glass of milk which I expect he will need more than milk to settle his stomach after he learns you are planning a wedding."

Uncle Roy turned to the foot shuffling young man and asked, "Are you sure you want to get into this family of lost prankster girls and a missing Granddad to boot? Marrying a girl who hides a pup in a big old black bag and thinks her little sister never pulls any of the pranks blamed on Daisy is pretty risky business!"

Don replied, "Oh, yes sir! Because we won't be around those concerns. We are going to live in Wyoming. That's why I wanted to get married next year. She can have one more year in Kansas with her family and friends. Grandmother Rosa needs her.

Roy said, "Smart young man. I expect you'll do and the family will accept you. Now that you are calling my Mother Grandmother Rosa already."

Then, Joe, the final Walker brother with his wife Hallie, son, Bud and daughter, Janice arrived. Hallie did all the talking. She explained how the entire trip from Burlingame, every radio station talked of the mysterious disappearance of a grandfather and his two granddaughters. After Hallie ran out of breath, Joe said, "Well, brothers, what have you learned? I never heard tell of three people disappearing so quickly and so completely off the face of the earth."

Janice having just graduated from high school and read every book in the library said, "You know a space ship was found in New Mexico right near Walker Mountain. The government refuses to talk about it. Maybe a space ship came here while they were on the porch. These space people are real small—just the size of Sharron and Daisy. Boy, if

34

Daisy tears into them they will return her real quick. She might make them bleed their green blood. Besides, they would never figure out her Texas drawl. I bet there is no language like that among all the planets. I say we just wait until they figure out that Texas Tornado will blow their space ship apart, and then we will find them by the noise.

Bud said, "Gosh Sis that is the silliest thing you have said during this whole trip. We know there are no flying saucers, no little space people with green blood, and no space languages. Besides, when I talked on the phone with Daisy, she said 'Oh Big Brother, I will not let anything keep me from seeing your newest steam train book. You will read it to us.' She was too excited to miss seeing me."

Grandmother said, "You are right, Bud. She even made a big secret deal about your coming to visit. She sang that song of hers, 'A tisket, a tasket, I've got a secret in my egg basket.' No, I agree they are somewhere around here real close by. Bud, what are you thinking? I can hear those Walker Wheels turning in your head. You know all the Walker men have those turning wheels in their heads. Especially when they are solving some problem, those wheels make much noise."

"Well, Grandmother, let's start at the first turn of the wheels" Bud said as he guided his Grandmother to the front porch "Here, Grandmother, sit in the rocking chair just like Granddad would have done. And if I know my tiny cousins; they played jacks on the porch. Daisy even said over the phone that Sharron had a new pig jacks game."

Grandmother joined in with, "Sharron was trying to teach her that new pig jacks game, but Daisy would have no part of it since she does not like pigs. So Sharron played jacks while Daisy jumped that piece of Texas lariat rope Roy had fixed for her. Then Grandmother explained she went into the house to see if Jenny and Christine needed anything for the meal they were preparing. After a bit, she returned to check on the girls as she could not hear them singing or playing. Only an empty front porch was to be found.

Bud said, "Um, Okay you know Granddad hand walks for those girls. Was he feeling up to hand walking? Then Bud walked down the sidewalk leading toward downtown. Suddenly he stopped, bent over, and picked up something shiny in a crack in the sidewalk. "A-ha!" he exclaimed. "I have found the old train conductors key which I gave to Granddad. It must have fallen out of his pocket. So he went right toward downtown. Oh, folks, you stay here in case they return. I have an idea where they might be. And it indeed is a sweet place to be in this heat."

"See, I told you his wheels were turning on a thought to find them! Our only grandson will solve the mystery of three missing family members, very shortly. We will have much to celebrate and be thankful for very soon.," said the excited Grandmother.

Then Christine touched Bud's left shoulder. She spoke slowly in her best deaf language so all could understand, knowing her speech was different. "Bud, those girls are everything to Jenny and me. Please, please find them. We have been praying so very hard for their safe return. It is not possible to lose them. It makes our hearts ache."

Bud hugged his aunts and nodded. With a twinkle in his eyes, he said, "Aunt Christine and Aunt Jenny, those little scamps will return to pull more pranks for many years with our family." Both aunts urged their tall handsome nephew to hurry and bring their daughters home.

Bud's sister, Janice said, "I think I'll go along to make sure you're not too hard on Granddad. Besides, I want to find Daisy so we can hike our skirts like we did last winter when Uncle Roy took our picture with his new camera. Her Texas laugh makes me smile and Sharron has the sweetest hugs. She is so special. This could be a real fun hide and seek sort of game."

Rose Mary scolded her sister for the vanity of skirt hiking. This caused their mother Hallie to interject, "Now girls! Don't quarrel! We have two lost tykes and a missing Granddad to think about. Off with you, Bud, Janice you may go to help him."

As Bud and Janice walked down Chautauqua Street toward Main Street, Janice asked, "Hey, Bud, what's your idea? Where are the girls and Granddad? Do you really have a clue? Or is this to calm down the folks?"

"Whoa, Sis! Your questions tumble over each other like the wheels on a Topeka, Hutcheson, and Santa Fe locomotive! Look on the sidewalk—more tokens, coins, and a coiled spring have fallen from Granddad's pockets." Now the brother and sister were at the corner.

As they looked to the right, a standing room only crown was gathered around the ice cream parlor. "I just wonder what that is all about?" mused Bud.

"Oh, Bud! You are just too curious and we don't need any ice cream since you brought the ice cream maker. We will make some later if we ever find those scamps!" growled Janice.

Bud noticed the crowd was unusually quiet. Then a local schoolteacher placed a finger to her lips to quell Janice's questions. Barely over the crowd's shuffling feet, Janice heard that all too familiar Texas drawl saying" . . . and then Uncle Nat said go down the cellar to get some of those canned Texas peaches. I said, 'NO! I am not gonna go down there with all those RAAAAAAATS hiding there after it rained last night. I do not like rats and hogs."

Janice could not hold back her joy, she yelled, "It's Daisy telling that infernal Rats in the Cellar story! How could everyone be interested in that? Has she told other tall Texas tales?"

Bud shushed his excited sister. He asked to be excused as he made his way through the crowd. Once inside the ice cream shop, he was so amazed he could not believe his eyes and ears. His Granddad was helping Mr. Widner serve the ice cream and count out the correct change from the antique cash register. Mr. Widner said, "Well sir, Mr. Walker that is the last of the ice cream. We are fresh out. I am so happy you helped me today. I have made more of a profit than any time since I opened this store. And I owe it all to you."

Granddad replied, "No, sir, Mr. Widner. It was those girls! Sharron and Daisy reading those stories out of the books in the corner. When they finished the stories, Sharron asked Daisy to tell her stories. That's what drew the crowd. They wanted to hear the made up stories. Boy, this has been a grand day. I just don't know when I have felt so, so, useful. Like I really did something."

Just then, Daisy ran to her Granddad and gave him a hug. She said, Granddad I am all out of stories."

He responded, "That is all right little Texas Wildflower. We are all out of ice cream. It is a perfect ending."

Then Sharron gave her Granddad a hug. She said, "You do know how to do things. Maybe, it is true, all you needed was some love and you could remember things. Oh, Granddad this is so good. I think everyone will be happy all this day."

The grandfather and the girls looked up to see Bud and Janice smiling at them. Daisy said, "Uh Oh Sharron we have had it for sure now. I bet we get our seats tanned over this! I am not scared. It was all fun. I will take your tanning and laugh about it."

Sharron said, "Oh, don't say that word . . . you know that word for bottoms, we are suppose to be nice. Now behave in front of all these folks. I just don't believe you might say it in front of them!"

Daisy replied, "Sharron-girl it is not a bad word. It is in the dictionary. I just dropped the ocks as it reminds me of the awful ham hOCKS. Phewy pigs!"

"I just don't believe you! We have to be nice. You are not afraid of anything or anyone." yelled Sharon.

Bud, sensing an all out tornado and earthquake about to happen, took each girl by the hand and asked, "You talked Granddad into hand walking to the ice cream shop? Was he well enough to do that?"

Daisy drawled, "NOOOOT eeexxaaactly. It was his idea but don't tell. As I don't want him to get into trouble. I will even take my tanning and Sharron's too. Granddad isn't too sick that love can't make him remember things. He has lots of fun in his heart."

"Tell you what, you two little scamps. Let's get you both and Granddad back home and we will deal with any punishments later.," said Bud with a grin.

The crowd at the ice cream parlor groaned together, "Oh No" at the thought of no more stories and empty ice cream tubs. Every one, reluctantly drifted down summery shimmery with heat sidewalks toward their homes. Mr. Widner cleaned his shop as he hummed a tune called Waltz Across Texas. His thoughts were happy ones. He wondered if that Walker bunch would be playing their guitars, violins, and mandolins after dark. He might just need to walk over and say his thanks again. Most likely, he would find his son Don hanging around that Alvena girl.

As Bud, Janice, Sharron and Daisy started down Chautauqua Street, Grandfather turned upside down to hand walk the remainder of the block home. Once again, he ignored his pockets emptying their contents with a jingling sound. Janice and the little tykes scrambled to collect his scattering treasures and tokens. They laughed at their Grandfather ignoring the clattering sounds of his falling treasures.

The Walker family heard the jingle jangle on the sidewalk and looked up to see their hand walking Grandfather. Janice was showing both little girls how to lift their skirts while pretending to be dancers. Bud said, Uncles, Dad, Aunts, Mother, and Grandmother we found them at Widner's Sweet Shoppe. It was crowded as it always is on a hot summer day. Granddad was helping Mr. Widner. All the ice cream buckets are empty and the antique cash register is full. I expect Mr. Widner will take all that cash home for safe stashing until the banks open."

Janice interrupted with, "Daisy was telling her Texas Tales because Sharron begged her to do. It was a sorta prank—after all there was no more ice cream in the for ice cream sundaes on Saturday. But everyone was still standing around."

Grandmother hurried from the porch as fast as her tiny feet would carry her. She drew herself up tall and faced her upside down husband's feet. She said, "Fool, hand walking at your age! Imagine YOU, leading those little girls to town. What excuse do you have for leaving the porch with Vernie and Fairy? Turn right side up while I am talking to you and stop being an embarrassment. Every church tomorrow will be a buzz about you and your antics."

The entire family fell into a silent state of shock. The Grandmother had never in over sixty years of marriage talked to her husband in such a stern manner. They were unsure how the headstrong patriarch of the Walker family would respond. It could be troubling. The dinner might not make it to a happy family around the large dining room table.

Grandfather turned right side up to face Grandmother's wrath. He grinned and said, "Why Rosa-girl, we just took a little stroll. Just my youngest granddaughters and me that is. Say, are you getting to be such an old woman who does not know the difference between your daughters and granddaughters? What's for supper? I have been smelling Texas fried chicken, mashed potatoes, cream gravy, and apricot cobbler all afternoon. My stomach is growling."

Daisy and Sharron said at the same time, "See Granddad knows us and all the family. We just took a little walk of love. He needs the love. Let's go eat before it gets cold. Let us go sit down on our bottoms real quick."

Granddad said, "And my little granddaughters are going to sit on either side of me so I won't get rib jabbed by some old woman". Then he winked at his sons.

The Walker family was so overjoyed to have their eldest and youngest members back in the fold. Any thoughts of punishment were forgotten. Sharron whispered to Daisy, "Boy, that, was a close call! We need to hurry up, sit down and be nice. Maybe they won't think of any spankings if we are sitting down next to Granddad. He would not let anyone punish us now."

Daisy grinned and said in her best drawl, "YA'll scardy cat! They aren't gonna switch us! We made Granddad remember stuff."

Later in the evening, Gene and Roy had played several songs on their guitars and mandolins. As dusk turned to dark cooling the scorching Kansas summer day, neighbors began to drift toward the Walker house. All wanted to hear the entire story of Granddad and his adventures with his granddaughters. A great golden moon rose in the sky. It cast a pleasant glow over the family and friends as the recalled memories told the neighbors of good times. The great adventure of a long ago wagon trip to New Mexico was recalled and the tale of Boys Searching for Melons had to be shared. Neighbors agreed the Walker bunch certainly had exciting experiences. One neighbor, a schoolteacher said the stories should be written for all to enjoy.

Sharron and Daisy sat on the ice cream bucket as each Walker cousin took turns at the crank. When the ice cream was near firm, Bud using his muscles turned the handle a few more times. Grandmother had her cookie pan ready to hold the dasher when it was removed. She promised her grandchildren could take turns tasting the cold dripping cream as it oozed off the dasher.

Fireflies began their light dances across the yard under the moon's soft glow. Roy said, "Sharron, Daisy put a drop of the ice cream on your fingers and the fireflies will sit on your fingers to eat the sweet cream. They will be like diamond rings on your fingers." The girls giggled at the thought of glowing golden rings. After a drop of the cream was placed on each finger, the girls slowly danced across the yard. They were softly singing, 'Come be my playmate, yell in my rain barrel, slide down my cellar door, go to town with my hand walking Granddad 'cause my Daddy is gonna get me many diamond rings.' With the last lyrics, the Walker family laughed at their tiny pranksters. Slowly the fireflies began to settle on the tiny sweetened fingers. Both girls stared in silent awe at the sparkling sight. They whispered, "This magic really makes us sister cousins forever more, more, more.

Their Grandmother softly called them to her. She whispered, "Now, I know what lasting gift I can give to each of you. Tomorrow, I'll teach you Sharron how to quilt and I'll teach you Daisy how to crochet. So forever more, more, more you can stitch and spin firefly shapes off your fingers. Besides, we have all been active today. A quiet day in my sewing room will be a treat. We can keep cool under the fan and know where each one of us is all day long."

When you see fireflies dancing in the golden light of a June moon, remember where you came from in your family. Know love keeps them laughing and laughing keeps them loving each other generation after generation after generation forever, more, more. A prankster or two helps the laugher to dance along its merry way among the hearts of one and all. Children, grandchildren, great grandchildren can continue to dance in love under firefly moons. This story needs not end here. You can tell your sweet memories to keep your own story alive and available to the next generation and the next generation and the next generation, forevermore.

The story did not end there. For five years later, Lawrence and Rosa's eleventh grandchild Leroy Evans Walker, II came into the family. He regrets having missed meeting his hand-walking grandfather who took his final hand walking to heaven in September 1949 the fall after the Firefly Moon family gathering.

"Lawrence, all Walkers have wheels turning in their heads instead of brains. Every Walker, I have met was born knowing how to fix machines, make music, write poetry, tell stories, make cookies, send a circle letter, or be a soldier." Rosa Margaret Klopfenstein Walker was a pioneer, strong spiritual survivor, role model, mentor, seamstress, cook, and inspiration to her subsequent generations of women to follow in her footsteps.

WHEELS: Mechanical, Music, Story, Cookie, Poetry, Soldier

The sturdy pioneer spirit of the Walker family flows through many generations. To capture some of their spirit this story is written to inspire new generations to reach deep within them to find their particular turning wheels; perhaps lying asleep in minds waiting for their hearts and souls to prime wheel turnings. As a beloved crocheted coverlet, the threads of the Walker DNA are colorful, strong, repeat patterns, endure, and bring smiles to the ones taking warm comfort under the memories of their individual stories. As with a warm coverlet, common threads run throughout the Walker family. These threads are military service to their beloved country, health service contributors of physicians, psychologist, nurses, hospice volunteers, and home health care providers. Joining the list are financial management services, bankers, musicians, writers, poets, researchers, teachers, engineers, inventors, kin seekers ranchers, hydrologists, geologists, farmers nurturing land, restless travelers with moving feet, adopting children, and various animals more like pets than work partners are found among all of the families. The most common thread is a chance for a good story, a grand laugh, and an opportunity to serve stand out among all the Walkers. The details of the adoptions, formal or informal, are unavailable to preserve privacy for the individual families. A deep generous love for children surges through the Walker DNA. By embracing the child, he or she is transforms into a Walker.

If dear reader you have made your way through *Boys Searching for Melons*, you will know Senator Nathanial Walker, known as Nat, was not born until well after Lawrence and Rosa returned to Kansas after nearly starving and thirsting through the dreadful drought of 1907. They were trying to coax a living from the land in Quay County New Mexico. Nat was a late in life baby born 1910 in Chautauqua County Kansas.

During his formative years, many tales floating through the family and among friends reveal he was an enterprising man. He trapped wild animals for food and fur skins, furthering the Walker skill of survival during difficult times. He repaired any kind of farm equipment with inherent mechanical knowledge. During oil was discovery around Elgin, Kansas, he also repaired the forever-breaking drilling equipment. He watched his older brother Leroy I (known as Roy) who loved the oil discovery business. Nat immediately knew how to repair the wooden oil drilling machines. The wooden machines quickly broke down due to inclement weather, inexperienced men known as rough necks, and poor material quality.

Nat invented and patented a gasoline converter to use kerosene, commonly known as coal oil during the waning days of World War II. Gasoline was in short supply but folks living in southern California needed to get to Camp Pendleton daily for their jobs. The kerosene converter saved the gasoline for the end of the war troops. Many an automobile was rescued from deterioration of idly sitting parked. Automobile wheels need to keep turning for proper functioning. **1**

Nat's supervisor and friend Snyder highly praised him for the innovative invention. He encouraged other Camp Pendleton workers to convert their automobiles so job goals could meet the national military regulations. After the close of the war, Captain James Pahl, Commanding Officer of the Naval Ammunitions Depot of Fallbrook, California recognized Nat for a Safety award for his suggestions on handling vans and trailers. **2**

Family stories say Nat was quite a prankster with his colleagues and his family. One of the pranks woven throughout Walker tales is the infamous bet between the brothers Roy and Nat. After the brothers had been fishing in the Red River on the northern border of Texas, Nat was irritated that his brother and friend Osage American Indian Sheriff Bruce chose to noodle for catfish in the skinny. To noodle for catfish is removing all on one's clothes, jumping into the deepest of pools, and reaching under rocks in the river to grasp large yellow catfish, which is excellent to eat. Nat repeatedly said it was so embarrassing to see his brother's white posterior sunny side up. To appease his younger brother, but mostly to stop Bruce from laughing himself silly, he placed a bet. The wager being each brother was to have a child born on the brother's respective birthdays. Nat did his part having a delightful Walker girl on his brother's birthday. However, Roy made Nat wait many decades until Roy's granddaughter Christina was born on Nat's birthday. For decades, the brothers needled each other on the bet. When Nat walked across the bridge of life, his brother Roy welcomed him with a hug and said, "Look, there in Texas is my third granddaughter born on your birthday, now the wage is off. You got here the day before my birthday. Besides, we cannot be pranking around in heaven." So both surrendered their wheel turning monkeyshines to more spiritual endeavors.

The brothers, Roy and Nat were blessed with the gifts of music by ear. While neither had formal music lessons, they could pick up any stringed instrument and play a song they had heard only once. Both loved to carry a harmonica for they often heard a new song on the radio. In their days, record players and vinyl records were in short supply due the rations of World War II. Family believes the brothers in heaven enjoy all the music they had missed on earth.

While Nat was the last child of the family, Roy was the second child. He was named Leroy Evans. His mother's family came from the Alsace Lorraine area of France. She thought Leroy meaning king in French was the appropriate name for her child. During the especially trying quest of a wagon trip in 1906 to Quay County, New Mexico, his mother was more sure of having named him correctly for his kingly leadership skills helped the family survive life harrowing experiences. Some of their experiences are in the story, *Boys Searching for Melons*.

Roy's wheel turnings led to a lifelong admiration for finely tuned automobiles. He invented a ramp made of hard woods so that he could easily make repairs to the undercarriage of his automobiles. While he never truly retired, he did leave his beloved wildcatter searches for oil to younger men with modern tools and geology training. He was proud of being asked to serve the military but was given honorable deferment to continue searching for oil for the troops. During what most men would call retirement, he devoted his wheel turning skills to keeping an automobile running so he could meet the educational needs of a teenage daughter and entering first grade son. He always carried a harmonica in his shirt pocket to capture a song recently heard. He claimed to have seen the first automobile at the turn of the twentieth century and the first man to walk on the moon via television. His love for children was endless. He appreciated a plentiful wheel turning well-lived life. He always had a fine horse or automobile with finely tuned horsepower. **3**

Roy's Cousin Fairy Pamelia Walker Lane was sixty days younger than him. Family stories relate they became close as teens while their families were in Quay County New Mexico during the family land claims of 1903-1906 around Walker Mountain. Their fathers were brothers known as J.A and L.C. Walker.

Fairy P. Walker Lane published over 200 poems under the writer's national number B-1787. After the twentieth century depression ruined the import business of The Fairy Hat and Gift Emporium **4** in Tucumcari, New Mexico, she moved to Ottawa, Kansas for a second career in nursing. During World War II, she studied nursing supervision at Kansas University. Then she worked a Pratt Whitney during the war years. She wrote poetry, children's stories, and magazine articles over a 45-year time span from 1940 to 1985. While Fairy wrote prior to 1940, no records of those writings remain. Some of her published poetry is included at the reference section of this story. The family continues the quest for her books *The Cherished Pony* and *Secrets of the Sea* published by Cook Publishers of Elgin, Illinois. The books are out of print and the publisher is searching for them. Fairy won the Eugene Field Society Award in 1946 and the National Association of Authors and Journalist

Poetry Biennial Award in 1976. She was a member of the Kansas Authors Club who recognized her many poems and short stories. **5**

Fairy's musical talents of singing and piano playing reflect the melodic skills threading through the Walker DNA strands. Her life long search for beauty was realized in her writing and music while caring for others. Her expressions of beauty seemed to come from another world, to quote William Lynch, a nephew in law. Mr. Lynch said Fairy had a vivid imagination leading her creative ability to be a poet.

Fairy's brother, Lytle Reese Walker, Sr. (L.R.) invented a flood detector for Southwest trains saving countless lives and millions of dollars of damage to equipment. He received no funds for the invention and wanted nothing more than to be of service. The device invented in 1915 was put into maximum application in 1933. L. R. Walker claimed to be a mere boy working out of Tucumcari, New Mexico when he noticed black rolling clouds in the sky. That meant flash floods. Nothing could stop the rains. In the Southwest, flashfloods filled arroyos and swept away cars and trains. The water would come out of the mountains in full momentum during cloudbursts. The torrents of water would rush down the arroyos with great force in walls of water. No warning to automobile drivers or train engineers existed. Although all indications of rain may have evaporated, a towering wall of water could be around a curve up the arroyo.

Until L.R. Walker invention of the flood detector, train engineers had no way of knowing if tracks were under water or trestles supports of bridges had washed out. The flood detector raises a float that in turn sets red lights in both directions along the track to warn engineers with sufficient time to bring a fast moving train to a safe stop. The detector functioned well for a 200-car train traveling 70 miles an hour. The manual detector was handset after triggering. Hand setting allowed inspection of the device for the next train's journey.

L. R. Walker was a train conductor for over half a century. At retirement, he said, "It was a beautiful ride." No doubt, his invention provided countless beautiful rides to numerous passengers and freight trains. However, his greatest gift was his only son defending our freedoms, Second Lieutenant Lytle Reese Walker, Jr., giving his life as a navigator of an airplane having gone down in the Pacific in 1946, just before the closing of World War II. **6**

Lawrence Ezra Walker another brother who also worked with the railroads loved the Quay County New Mexico Walker homesteads. In particular, he loved a special mountain named Walker Mountain. In his youth, he carved his initials LEW in a cave of his beloved mountain. While documents of this mountain have long ceased to exist, the Walkers of today are seeking to authenticate its name with the appropriate governmental channels. The family does not seek to own the land or mineral rights. Claiming the Walker heritage of loving a mountain that sheltered them in its cave early twentieth century is sufficient. Walker pioneers were seeking to work the land for a living. Lawrence Ezra wrote poems to honor his beloved mountain, more of a huge mound than a mountain but his love for this land made the mountain large in his point of view. Now his large love of the mountain has made its way to more generations. **7**

Emory Clair Walker, Sr., another brother faced challenges that few men could endure. With dignity, distinguished style, dedicated devotion and loving care, he nurtured a 19-month-old son and 3-day-old daughter. Their mother walked across the bridge of life due to birthing complications. With dependable assistance from the children's maternal grandparents, Emory, Sr. met each daily experience for nearly 5 years before marrying again. His Walker DNA indicates many threads of strength. He too had a harmonica collection to capture tunes to cheer his soul.

When Emory Clair, Sr. was 8 years old in 1908 he attended the Bonita school 5 miles southwest of Tucumcari, New Mexico. The teacher was his 16-year old sister, Miss Evalina Walker Hammond. The 10 students pictured vary in age. Miss Evalina taught her brother and two sisters during their elementary education days. Miss Walker also taught at the Walker School named after her father J.A. Walker. **8, 9, 10**

Emory C. Walker, Jr. son of Emory C. Walker, Sr. lives a unique and richly blessed life. He considers his five years of Army life as a reward of good memories. On June 15, 1953, Emory was holding onto the sides of a trench during a Chinese barrage on Out Post Harry during the Korean War. He was wounded. After his surgery in Osaka, Japan, he sang The Eyes of Texas as he was recovering from the anesthesia. Fourteen surgeries and two bone grafts later, Emory celebrated the saving of his arm and hand. He was bestowed with a Purple Heart for his heroic efforts. **11**

Emory retired from the Colorado National Bank as Trust Officer, a suitable title for a Purple Heart honoree. Since 1988, he volunteers at the Visitor Center of the Denver Metro Convention and Visitor Bureau. He enjoys telling people where to go and how to get there as an Ambassador at Denver International Airport. He also enjoys his volunteer work at a homeless day shelter, St. Francis Center and being a tour guide at the Colorado State Capital. He has spent time as a court friend for the Denver Probate Court. St. Luke's Episcopal Church is another important part of his ever giving to others life. Currently he is nurturing and cherishing an ailing family member.

Emory provides endless Walker family research data to all the branches of Walker cousins. He has motivated and encouraged the writing of the Walker Trilogy. It is through Emory, the researcher found other cousins heretofore unknown. When a person brings family together, he has walked the paths designed by God.

Emily Abigail Walker Henson was a sophisticated dinner party hostess of Sedan, Kansas during the years of 1871-1927. She was a dearly loved pioneer resident. She often assisted ill and suffering people when trained nurses were unavailable . . . All cherished her skills during times of sickness. She is the eldest sister to J.A. and L.C. Walker.

Mrs. Henson raised six children, two sons and four daughters. Her sons preceded her in the walk across the bridge of life. Her appreciation of a beautiful life was passes onto her daughters and their husbands. Her love of beauty found expression in the flowers surrounding her home and her daughters, which are striking beauties in their tintypes photographs.

Mrs. Henson's father, Walter Baker Walker was a pastor throughout Kansas. Most likely, the spiritual life early on influenced her, as she professed her faith in Christ at the age of 14. A host of friends and family carry this in her memory:

Life's race well run,
Life's work well done
Life's crown well won,
Now comes the rest.

Mrs. Henson's great grandson Dr. R.J. Black Henson served as a physician in the United States Military for decades. He shares that a family friend retired from the Navy told many stories about world travels and experiences. These stories appealed to his aspirations for travel. In 1950, Dr. Henson graduated high school and attempted to join the Navy. He was rejected which created a serious blow to his psyche. He went to college becoming a professional student, as many of the Walker family have become lifelong students.

When he was in medical school, the army drafted him. Through negotiations, he influenced the Air Force to make the switch from Army. This is a typical Walker characteristic; go after what is wanted. Dr. Henson's first assignment was Wright Patterson in research. Then he was sent to Walter Reed for his internship. He was assigned to flight surgeons school; next onto England for three years. He had one top-secret flight that still is written about today 52 years later. He has the story on file. He spent 4 years in San Antonio, Texas for orthopedic surgery training, 2 years at Scott Air Force Base taking care of casualties from Vietnam, and 1 year in Can Tho near Binh Thuy Air Force Base. 223 hours of combat flying time is a part of his military history. Dr. Henson received the Commendation Medal, the Bronze Star, Air Medal, and a Star on his wings badge for promotion to senior flight surgeon, then promoted to Colonel, and awarded Legion of Merit at retirement.

In his retirement, he is researching the Walker and Henson family genealogy lines and stories. He is a thought-provoking conversationalist. He travels about with his beloved pug, Meiko, visiting cousins and researching the Walker and Henson stories. The dog breed pug appeals to the Walker sense of discipline, persistence, intelligence, and playfulness. It is not surprising to know Dr. Henson has chosen the pug as his mascot and charming traveling partner.

Dr. Henson's brother, John Edward Henson, PhD was a retired professor emeritus of Chemistry, teaching 38 years at Westminster College. He also served as associate dean and head of the computer center. Keeping the tradition of Westminster, he functioned as Marshall and sponsor of the Skulls of Seven for 30 years. He served in the Army Chemical Corps, serving at Aberdeen Proving Grounds and Edgewood Arsenal in Maryland. He was a beloved man of many talents including chef, woodwork, puzzle solver, avid bridge player, master gardener including a greenhouse and water feature with waterfall and fish. He was born March 5, 1936 in Nowata, Oklahoma and crossed the bridge of life April 20, 2013. His many talents reflect Walker DNA. Those who have been honored to know him miss him greatly; those not fortunate enough to have had their Walker spirits touched by him, regret their loss. His wife and high school sweetheart Mary Jane Love, three children and six grandchildren survive him.

Deanna Carolyn Lynch Wright, niece to Fairy Pamelia Walker Lane daughter of Fairy Angelina Hammond Lynch (known as Little Fairy) and granddaughter of Evalina Mae Walker Hammond, great granddaughter of Joseph Anson (JA) Walker and Effie Mae Carpenter Walker, carries the enterprising Walker threads in her DNA.

Dreaming of a farm, Carolyn and Doug Wright bought land with a much needing renovations two-story farmhouse outside of Little River, Kansas. The original wood floors remain to creak when folks walk. The floors are singing songs of generations of happy families created therein since 1911. When one visits Carolyn's home, the century plus structure, reflects immense love and amazing spiritual presences. The dining room walls seem to fill with overflowing warm love much, as a waterfall would continually bring refreshing waters for the soul. The upstairs hall echoes the joyful laughter of children adrift in their playfulness. As the Kansas light filters through the leaves of the tress, lacy patterns dance on the walls.

She lost her high school sweetheart husband Doug in a 1998. When Doug walked across the bridge of life, he left his spirit in the form of a guardian essence in their bedroom. Carolyn's soaring indomitable undefeated spirit is buoyed by her love of the sea. Perhaps due to overwhelming numbers of sailor's in her family tree or possibly due to her love of soothing salty water or perchance the guardian angel is her life anchor.

In 1992, she began the Little Ol' Cookie House with the business name of CBC Foods, Inc. out of her historic farmhouse kitchen. Later she moved to a small house in Little River, Kansas. Now she operates her food manufacturing business in Little River, Kansas on Main Street. Her woman owned business had the most productive year in 1998, making one to wonder did her beloved's spirit guided her, as a captain would steer his ship across the sea. Carolyn is blessed with three sons who encourage her business enterprise. Two sons work daily with her to make sure Carolyn has opportunities for the creative side of the business, while they focus on the daily organization and management matters. Carolyn was awarded the Woman Owned Business of the Year for the state by the Kansas Commerce Department as is cited in The Topeka Capital Journal October 28, 2003. **12**

The Better Business Bureau ranks CBC Foods, Inc. as A+ with no complaints, ever. Moreover, Carolyn's cookies taste swell as well as being a great fund raising project for schools, churches or other organizations. Her website www.cookiehouse.com is a delightful place to visit via the internet. **13**

The Walker military men have given much to secure the freedoms we enjoy today. Dr. Henson treated the casualties of Viet Nam. Another gave his life in World War II and remains missing since January 5, 1946. Two others came away from World War I with deeply wounded bodies or spirits. Sparse military documentation is available.

Louis F. Walker, PVT enlisted May 22, 1918 and was separated from the army February 8, 1919 after suffering permanent disablement from gas while serving in Battery E, 56 Field Artillery, 19 Div. and Troop E, 309 Cavalry. He was 24 years old. Census records report his was married less than a decade from 1921 to 1930. Apparently, no children were born to this marriage. No family, to date, has records of this marriage. He lived with family or in national homes for disabled soldiers. He suffered the debilitating injuries until his death December 11, 1961. While he remained alive in the medial definition, he was dead in the spiritual and psychological definitions. In effect, he gave his life to defend the USA in World War I. He is interred at Ft. Bliss National

Cemetery. Rest in peace cherished soldier, you paid the ultimate price for our freedoms.

Lawrence Ezra Walker poet and carver of the LEW initials in the cave of Walker Mountain served in the army. He desired no discussions on his military experiences. Family narratives speculate he may have witnessed abhorrent trench warfare in France. One wonders if he concentrated on his beloved Walker Mountain to outlast the horrors of World War I. Military records reflect his service from June 21, 1915 to March 1919. He entered as a Private First Class and separated with honors as a Corporal. His internment is at Fort Bliss National Cemetery not far from his brother Louis F. Walker. Rest in peace treasured soldier, you paid a vast cost for our liberties.

Lawrence Hall Walker son of Lawrence Ezra served in the Navy for about two years.

Sketchy military records show him on board the USS Lexington a CV-16. He was sailing from SASEBO, Japan via Pearl Harbor onto USA April 15, 1946. His views of the Pacific theater must have been linear in reverse five years after the assault on Pearl Harbor. He was discharged August 16, 1946. He lived in west Texas. He must have found it amusing his ship is a floating museum in Corpus Christi, Texas. Thank you, Hall for your service guarding our freedoms to country, Texas and family.

Lytle R. Walker, Jr., Second Lieutenant U.S. Army Air Forces, Second Air Sea Rescue Squadron holds the Killed in Action Status. He won seven Battle Stars, held the Air Medal with one Cluster, Presidential Citation, P.I. Liberation Ribbon and other honors as shown by limited military records. The War Department declared January 5, 1946 as his date of death. His obituary states he died in an airplane crashed in the Philippine Islands while he was serving with the Second Emergency Rescue Squadron, known as the "Snafu Snatchers". The word SNAFU meaning Situation Normal All Fouled Up lends meaning to their assigned missions. The squadron was famous for rescuing downed aviators in the seas around the Philippines. This was a morale building squadron in that their mission was to rescue troops rather than kill them. Even so, in rescue attempts, the enemy often fires upon those in rescue from the Pacific or even worse, tried to take down the rescue squadrons. In less than a year, 54 men were escaped harsh Pacific waters in and out of enemy territory. His last known letter home reveals a professional soldier looking forward to the war ending and returning to Texas. His picture presents a strong handsome man. His dreams ceased far too soon. His parents, six-year-old daughter, Sharron Ann and her mother Aileen, survived him. His memorial of honor is Fort Bonifacio, Manila, Philippines Wall of Missing. As your airplane was going down, you must have grabbed a hand full of stars to pass out to the Walkers in or coming to heaven. Rests well in peace, precious soldier, you have paid the supreme price to secure the independence for USA, Texas and family. **14, 15, 16, 17**

Emory C. with the Purple Heart honor, indeed your story is here, well almost.

Due to your assistance and inspirational memories, honors and dedication is given to the Walker men of this story. These stories will be donated to the Daughters of the American Revolution Library in Washington D.C., celebrating all the Walker Women who have supported and loved the Walker Men. In other places, a Walker Military Memories is being established. Your encouraging jubilation in finding Walker Mountain and Walker School will lead to other Walker Stories. Emory it is your joyous sharing of materials, which kept the writing wheels turning to the completion and publication of the Walker Trilogy. During the times of dry research, your emails, telephone calls, and pony express mail triggered the writing quill to start writing, once again. For this and so much more, you are part of the significant Walker military men.

One might inquire with the proliferation of male Walker children, who lives today to carry on the Walker name? In particular, the duplication of the names Lawrence and Fairy, which were popular names in previous century, do not surface in modern times. Research reveals Leroy Evans Walker, II and his son Leroy Evans Walker, III, both of Burkburnett, Texas and Gary Walker of San Angelo, Texas and Robert (Bobby) Walker of Fresno, California, Texas sons of Lawrence Hall Walker are appointees to carry on the Walker name. Leroy II says he has completed his assignment and his interests focus on the Walker Cousin making those grand cookies coming out of the Little Ol' Cookie House and exploring Walker Mountain.

This abstract of Walker Heritage stories gives a miniature sample the richly filled well-lived lives. Their ability to survive near starvation, droughts, injuries, loss of children, epidemics, property losses, and countless other trials of life strengthened their DNA and genes which that have passed onto new generations grateful for the survival genes. The Walkers come from humble modest disciplined lifestyles. They rose by force of their natural genius. Obstacles in their life's pathways served to rouse latent strengths. They set aside their discouragements to attain their focused goals. Looking at the past, we can see what the future holds. The admirable Walker DNA will carry through many generations of the male and female Walkers.

Gentle reader, as you enjoy *Under the Firefly Moon* know that it took many generations of living, just living well, to arrive at that summer of 1949 when the last of the Ancient Walkers gathered to celebrate the next generation. A generation, which was given so much while so little, was expected of them. Then again, those who loved where they came from, honor, respect, cherish and carry forth the undefeatable and formidable Walker Heritage.

Most of the selected Walker stories come from a time of doing what is right for it felt grand to do so. Today doing what is correct puts one in a tiny minority. It is peaceful in that minority. Seemingly, anything that turns, goes round or is circular attracts the Walkers. Wagon wheels, train wheels, water well pulley wheels, oil well drilling rigs, medical equipment for healing such as stethoscopes, military medals, circle letters, cookies, pies, bicycles, motor bikes, circular poems, even the round Walker Mountain in Quay County New Mexico, circumnavigating travels, love surrounding children, seniors, and stories told all around. The honorable heritage the Walkers have bestowed upon us 21st century kinfolks is most valuable. Let these Walkers and their meanderings amble through your souls and hearts and share the stories with others in your lineage.

Documentation Appendix

PERSONS	DESCRIPTION
Lawrence C. Walker 11 Nov 1863 Sunrise 22 Sep 1949 Sunset	**Father** of Leck, Leroy I, Glee, Joe, Nat, Vernie, Fairy, Clisty; **Brother** of Emily Abigail Walker Henson; **Uncle** of Fairy P. Walker Lane, Lytle R. Walker, Sr., Evalina J. Walker Hammond, Louis F. Walker, Lawrence Ezra Walker, Emory C. Walker, Sr.; **Grand Uncle** of Lytle R. Walker, Jr., Lawrence Hall Walker, Emory C. Walker, Jr.; **Great Grand Uncle** to Dr. RJ Black Henson, John E. Henson, PhD, Deanna Carolyn Lynch Wright, Gary Walker **Grandfather** of Leroy Walker. II; Daisy A. Walker Palmer, PhD, Lois Walker Koontz, Helen Walker Ryan, Jeanette Walker Stotts, Alvena Walker Widner, Sharon Walker Williams, Jeanne Walker Taylor, Janice Walker Roberts, Joseph Walker, and Rosemary Walker Rockey **Great Grandfather** Leroy Walker, III, Christina Walker Doest, Christy Yazdi, Cyndi Seven

Senator Nathaniel Walker
27 Apr 1910 Sunrise
14 Jun 1994 Sunset

Son of Lawrence C and Rosa Walker; **Brother** of Leck, Leroy I. Glee, Joe, Nat, Vernie, Fairy, Clisty; **Nephew** of Emily Abigail Walker Henson; **Cousin** of Fairy P. Walker Lane, Lytle R. Walker, Sr., Evalina J. Walker Hammond, Louis F. Walker, Lawrence Ezra Walker, Emory C. Walker, Sir; **Second Cousin** of Lytle R. Walker, Jr., Emory C. Walker, Jr, Lawrence Hall Walker.; **Third Cousin** of Dr. RJ Black Henson, John E. Henson, PhD, Deanna Carolyn Lynch Wright, Gary Walker; **Uncle** of Leroy II; **Grand Uncle** Leroy III. **Father** of Alvena Mae Walker Widner, Sharron Doris Walker Williams. **Grandfather** of Glenn Ward, James Ward, Celeste Ward Higby, Terry Widner, Sue Widner McClintock.

Leroy Evans Walker, I
15 Jun 1890 Sunrise
13 Aug 1970 Sunset

Son of Lawrence C. and Rosa Walker; **Brother** of Leck, Glee, Joe, Nat, Vernie, Fairy, Clisty; **Nephew** of Emily Abigail Walker Henson; **Cousin** of Fairy P. Walker Lane, Lytle Walker, Sr., Evalina J. Walker Hammond, Louis F. Walker, Lawrence Ezra Walker, Emory C. Walker, Sr.; **Second Cousin** of Lytle R. Walker, Jr., Emory C. Walker Jr.; Lawrence Hall Walker; **Third Cousin** of Dr. RJ Black Henson, John E. Henson, PhD, Deanna Carolyn Lynch Wright, Gary Walker; **Father** of Leroy II, Daisy Ann Walker Palmer, PhD; **Grandfather** of Leroy III, Christy Ann Yazdi, Cyndi Ann Seven, Christina Lucille Walker Doest, **Great Grandfather** of Dylan Doest, Heather Walker, Jason Guyn, Starla Thornhill, and Justin Thornhill.

Fairy P. Walker Lane 11 Sep 1890 Sunrise 27 Feb 1985 Sunset	**Niece** of Emily Abigail Walker Henson, Lawrence C. Walker; **Cousin** of Leck, Leroy I, Glee, Joe, Nat, Vernie, Fairy, Clisty, **Sister** of Lytle R. Walker, Sr., Evalina J. Walker Hammond, Louis F. Walker, Lawrence Ezra Walker, Emory C. Walker, Sr.; **Aunt** of Lytle R. Walker, Jr, Emory C. Walker, Jr, Lawrence Hall Walker; **Grand Aunt** of Deanna Carolyn Lynch Wright, Gary Walker; **Second Cousin** of Leroy II; **Third Cousin** of Dr. RJ Black Henson, John E. Henson, PhD., Leroy III.
Lytle Reese Walker, Sr. 21 Apr 1887 Sunrise 25 Oct 1982 Sunset	**Nephew** of Emily Abigail Walker Henson, Lawrence C. Walker; **Cousin** of Leck, Leroy I, Glee, Joe, Nat, Vernie, Fairy, Clisty; **Brother** of Fairy P. Walker Lane, Evalina J. Walker Hammond, Louis F. Walker, Lawrence Ezra Walker, Emory C. Walker, Sr.; **Uncle** of Emory C. Walker, Jr., Lawrence Hall Walker; **Grand Uncle** of Deanna Carolyn Lynch Wright, Gary Walker; **Second Cousin** of Leroy II; **Third Cousin** of Dr. RJ Black Henson, John E. Henson, PhD., Leroy III; **Father** of Lytle R. Walker, Jr. and Carolyn Sue Walker Weaver.
Lytle Reese Walker, Jr. 18 Dec 1916 Sunrise 5 Jan 1946 Sunset	**Son** of Lytle Reese Walker, Sr.; **Brother** of Carolyn Sue Walker, Weaver; **Grand Nephew** of Emily Abigail Walker Henson, Lawrence C. Walker; **Nephew** of Fairy P. Walker Lane, Evalina J. Walker Hammond, Louis F. Walker, Lawrence Ezra Walker, Emory C. Walker Sr.; **Cousin** of Emory C. Walker, Jr, Lawrence Hall Walker; **Second Cousin** of Gary Walker, Leck, Leroy I, Glee, Joe, Nat, Vernie, Clisty, Fairy; **Third Cousin** of Deanna Carolyn Lynch Wright, Leroy II, **Fourth Cousin** of Leroy III; Dr. R.J. Black Henson, John E. Henson, PhD.; **Father** of Sharon Ann Walker Brett.

Louis Floyd Walker
30 Sep 1894 Sunrise
11 Dec 1961 Sunset

Nephew of Emily Abigail Walker Henson, Lawrence C. Walker, **Cousin** of Leck, Leroy I, Glee, Joe, Nat, Vernie, Fairy, Clisty; **Brother** of Fairy P. Walker Lane, Evalina J. Walker Hammond, Lawrence Ezra Walker, Emory C. Walker, Sr.; **Uncle** of Emory C. Walker, Jr., Lawrence Hall Walker; **Grand Uncle** of Deanna Carolyn Lynch Wright, Gary Walker; Second Cousin of Leroy II; **Third Cousin** of Dr. R.J Black Henson, John E. Henson, PhD, Leroy III.

Lawrence Ezra Walker
7 Jan 1897 Sunrise
12 Jun 1983 Sunset

Nephew of Emily Abigail Walker Henson, Lawrence C. Walker; **Cousin** of Leck, Leroy I, Glee, Joe, Nat, Vernie, Fairy, Clisty; **Brother** of Fairy P. Walker Lane, Evalina J. Walker Hammond, Louis F. Walker, Lawrence Ezra Walker, Emory C. Walker, Sr., Lytle R. Walker, Sr.; **Uncle** of Emory C. Walker, Jr., Lawrence Hall Walker; **Grand Uncle** Deanna Carolyn Lynch Wright, Gary Walker; **Second Cousin** of Leroy II; **Third Cousin** of Leroy III; Dr. JR Black Henson, John E. Henson, PhD.; **Father** of Doris B. Walker Bullock, Lawrence Hall Walker, June E. Walker Hollenshead, Velma G. Walker Coleman, Dr. Marilyn J. Walker, Marvin Zane Walker.

Lawrence Hall Walker
31 Oct 1926 Sunrise
30 Jun 2013 Sunset

Son of Lawrence Ezra Walker; **Great Nephew** of Emily Abigail Walker Henson, Lawrence C. Walker; **Nephew** of Fairy P. Walker, Lane, Evalina J. Walker Hammond, Louis F. Walker, Emory C. Walker, Sr. ; **Cousin** of Lytle Reese Walker, Jr.; **Second Cousin** of Leck, Leroy I, Glee, Joe, Nat, Vernie, Fairy, Clisty; **Third Cousin** of Deana Carolyn Lynch Wright Leroy II; **Fourth Cousin** of Leroy III; **Father** of Gary Walker and Robert (Bobby) Walker.

Emory C. Walker, Sr.
31 Mar 1900 Sunrise
12 Sep 1975 Sunset

Nephew of Emily Abigail Walker Henson, Lawrence C. Walker; **Cousin** of Leck, Leroy I, Glee, Joe, Nat, Vernie, Fairy, Clisty; **Brother** of Fairy P. Walker Lane, Evalina J. Walker Hammond, Louis F. Walker, Lawrence Ezra Walker, Lytle R. Walker, Sr.; **Uncle** of Lawrence Hall Walker; **Grand Uncle** of Deanna Carolyn Lynch Wright, Gary Walker; **Second Cousin** of Leroy II; **Third Cousin** of Leroy III; Dr. JR Black Henson, John E. Henson, PhD; **Father** of Emory C. Walker, Jr., Mary Kathryn Walker Cooley and Sara Sue Walker.

Emory C. Walker, Jr.
11 Sep 1929 Sunrise

Son of Emory C. Walker, Sr.; **Great Nephew** of Emily Abigail Walker Henson, Lawrence C. Walker; **Nephew** of Fairy P. Walker Lane, Evalina J. Walker Hammond, Louis F. Walker, Lawrence Ezra Walker, Lytle R. Walker, Sr.; **Cousin** of Lytle R. Walker, Jr., Lawrence Hall Walker; **Second Cousin** of Leck, Leroy I, Glee, Joe, Nat, Vernie, Fairy, Clisty; **Third Cousin** of Deanna Carolyn Lynch Wright, Leroy II; **Fourth Cousin** of Leroy III; **Father** of Nancy Walker and Judy Walker Green.

The persons listed are in one of the three stories. The family extraction is for the ease of the reader to relate to flow of the story and the placement of a particular Walker. Those not listed are not being ignored. Either information is insufficient, late in coming to the researcher, or they are not integral to the chronicles at this point. They could show up in future stories. Anyone wanting to share additional information with the researcher author would be most welcomed. At the near completion of this Trilogy, the researcher was informed a second cousin down the Walker line wished to also write family stories. It is heartening that others see the value of family stories.

Epilogue

The Lawrence C. Walker family enjoyed Walker Mountain along with the Lytle Walker and Lawrence Ezra Walker families. (Lawrence and Lytle were brothers). Later a severe drought found the land could not support the families. The Lawrence C. Walker family returned to Kansas to round out their family of five boys and three girls. The last child, Senator Nathaniel was born April 27, 1910. The tiny mother cherished all family matters and held the precious memories in her heart. She chose to remember only the good and dear recollections. She would live to see nine granddaughters and two grandsons. All of whom wish they had collected more of the golden family stories from Rosa Margaret Klopfenstein Walker.

To this day, Walker Mountain shelters the LEW initials. The giggles of the Walker children are dancing on the winds blowing through Quay County. Some of Rosa and Lawrence's grandchildren have taken a quest to have Walker Mountain and recently discovered Walker School named after Joseph Anson (J.A) Walker evidenced with a historical marker. It remains to be if the 21st Century of multiplicity of governmental red tape procedures can survive the persistence of those Walker cousins.

As for the reading sewing glasses of Sarah Jane Kirk Klopfenstein, mother of Rosa Margaret Klopfenstein Walker, they made their way to Roy. Roy's daughter has them framed in a heritage shadow box titled: Keys to the Past. It is hangs on a wall opposite Sarah Jane's Victorian Crazy Quilt Pillow Sham in a museum frame. The story, *Found: A Quilt Hanging in a Family Tree* is about Sarah Jane's 126-year-old quilt and is in the Daughters of the American Revolution Library in Washington D. C. with the Clisty Jane Walker Story of 1892. A Kirk, Klopfenstein, Walker file is in the library for more family stories where the *Walker Trilogy* will be available for researchers to enjoy.

① Gasolene Carburetor directly below.
② Fuel Carburetor   "   ".
③ Vaporizer Unit.
④ Vapor intake to Engine

1

L-294-1N. Capt. James H. Pahl, Commanding Officer, Naval Ammunition Depot, Fallbrook, California, presenting $115.00 safety award to Senator Walker, Diesel Equipment Mechanic, Transportation Division, for his suggestion on the steps and handle arrangement on covered vans and trailers.

Leroy Evans Walker, I 1890 — 1970

3

4

Fairy Pamelia Walker Lane Poems Collected from Kansas Authors Club and Yearbook, Kansas State Historical Society Library, and Ideals Magazine. Much appreciation is given to Don Stuart Prady researcher with the Kansas Historical Society for his diligent search among the archives to bring forth these poems.

In Forest Depth

Moonlight cannot penetrate.
Darkness resigns supreme
In forest depth—and it is good.
For one can meditate and dream.

Forgotten are life's many trials,
In the quiet depth of the great trees;
The sense of peace and rest abounds,
Gradually all pressures ease.

And one can search his inmost soul,
And place true values high and clear;
Beyond the petty trials of life,
And thereby conquer self and fear.

Then step forth a better man,
For having dwelt in forest dark—
And spent soul-searching hours
To find the vital, living spark.

Fairy Walker Lane Page 24 of
Kansas Authors Club 1956
Poetry Anthology

Spirit of America

America, we cherish you,
Dear homeland that we love;
We shall defend our liberty,
Though foes may boast of
    mighty power,
Defeat, we will not see;
For the Spirit of America
Is one of victory.

Fairy Walker Lane 1973
entire work sent to President
Richard Nixon, complete work
remains undiscovered in 2013

Life's Pathway

Tread softly o'er life's pathway 'tis sacred ground you tread;
God wished man to be happy—(cant souls of men be dead?)
He provided the great rich earth and flowing rivers free;
Pink sunrise and golden moon, gay flowers and deep blue seas,
We sit midst in a great torn world, the land in fear is trod—
Who has failed along the way—think you—'tis man—or God?

Fairy E. Lane (Fay carpenter) Ottawa, Kansas 1940
Kansas Authors Club Quotation Year book
{Seeming, she was changing her name or using a pen name}

Consolation

Out where the wind whispers softly
Among the festoons of green,
Out in the blue open spaces
Where a flash of scarlet is seen;

Far off in a veiled horizon
Beyond the flowering hills,
Down in the verdant valley,
Out where a wild bird trills;

Where Lady June calls and beckons
With irresistible charm;
To a dream-world, clam and mystic,
Far removed from chaos and harm;

Let us heed June's call from the valley,
Let us heed June's call from the hill;
Immerse our souls in her beauties,
Till our beings with rapture thrill.

Let sorrow melt and vanish,
And fear on swift wings arise;
In the tranquil peace and freedom
Of god's great paradise!

Fairy Walker Lane 1944 Yearbook
Authors Club

Friendship's Golden Chain

I caught the far-flung, sacred loop
Of friendship's golden chain;
It sang unto a lonely heart
A touching, sweet refrain
Of kindly thoughts in golden links
And pleasant memories;
That bind us closer day by day,
To calm life's troubled seas.
The golden lining to life's cloud,
Magically overspread,
Illumined the spark of happiness
On woven, gilded thread.
May friendship's golden chain remain
Throughout the coming years;
And may each tiny link impress
The thought friendship endears!

Fairy Walker Lane 1948 Kansas
Yearbook Authors Club page 67

Winter's Hush

Winter's hush is on the land
Where Spring lies lost in sleep;
The singing brooks of summer days
No more in ripples leap;
The sun is cold, the sky is gray,
The hills are wrapped in snow;
Fierce is the wind that blows a gale,
Gone is the sunset's glow.

The forest trees stand stark and bare
And no sweet songster's voice
Flings melody with tuneful art,
To make the heart rejoice.
The lake in covered sheet of ice
Reflects no willow's lace;
There are no purple violet
The forest floor to grace.

All is hushed and quiet here,
O'er hill and wood and lake—
As if they fear, with bated breath,
The sleeping Spring to wake!

Fairy Walker Lane 1945 Kansas Authors Yearbook

6

Spring Beauty

Have you felt that thrill of pleasure
  When May flowers were in bloom;
When the land was crowned by Springtime
  Just released from Winter's tomb?
Have you walked upon god's carpet
  So magically spread;
With Spring beauty interwoven,
  Gay with vari-colored thread?
Have you stood before your Maker
  Shorn of ego and of greed;
Felt your spirit rise and answer
  His response, in hour of need?
Have you felt that thrill of pleasure
  Deep within your inmost soul;
With faith to meet life's daring challenge,
  With hope renewed in cherished goal?
Then your life will be far richer,
  And respond like glorious Spring;
Spreading beauty of your spirit
  In footsteps of your King!

Fairy Walker Lane 1947 Kansas
Authors Club page 60

Chippeway's Dancing Leaves

On the Chippeway Hills are Gypsy leaves
To dance when the autumn wind blows;
All costumed in scarlet and brown and gold,
They dance around on their toes.

They're dancing over the hills tonight,
Whirling, 'round, side by side—
Their ball room is the forest floor
Where ghosts of Chippeways ride.
While the night wind plays requiem
For the warrior of by-gone days—
The Gypsy leaves dance 'round on their toes
To the music of autumn wind plays!

Fairy Walker Lane 1950 Kansas Authors Club
Yearbook page 59 Written in memory of the Chippeway Indians
Who once inhabited the Chippeway Hills south of Ottawa, Kansas

Ode To A Meadow

To alien eyes the beauty of you
May only be a passing view;
But to me, you're a meadow of
  pure delight
Where wild flowers are nodding
  gay and bright,
And tall trees shield the herd
  from the sun,
Where laughing water, in small
  brooks run;
And Cardinals trill as they
  lightly sway,
And mushrooms spring at the
  break of day.
Strawberries, red and lush abound
In clusters on the dew-kissed ground;
The depth of the magic wading pool
Reflects a minows' swimming school.
Where days were spent happy and free
As a butterfly flitting over the lea.
But childhood claims you, and
  I must stay
In a world of chaos—and yet, I stray
Into the glow of sweet memory
Always to fine serenity.

Fairy Walker Lane 1954 Kansas
Authors Club Yearbook page54

El Paso Post 4-21-76 L.R. Birthday = 89.

El Pasoan invented flood detector for Southwest trains

By BETTY PIERCE

A device invented by an El Paso man in 1915 has saved countless lives and prevented perhaps millions

L.R. WALKER

of dollars worth of damage to equipment, but has paid no royalties to the inventor.

"I didn't want anything

for it," said L.R. Walker, of 2925 Altura avenue. "I just wanted to save the lives of my friends, and property.

"I WAS JUST a boy, working out of Tucumcari, and when I saw the black clouding rolling in the sky, I knew it meant flash floods, and that there was nothing to stop the rains."

In the Southwest, flash-floods may fill an arroyo and sweep away a car or a train in an area in which there has been no rain. The water comes out of the mountains, gathering momentum during a cloudburst, and rushing down the arroyos with great force.

Experienced automobile drivers in this part of the country, when dark clouds top the mountains and the

must drive through an arroyo, stop and listen for the sound of rushing water before entering the floor of the arroyo to cross. They know that while there may be no rain where they are, a towering wall of water may be just around the curve up the arroyo.

UNTIL MR. WALKER

invented his flood detector, there was no way for an engineer to know whether the track was underwater, or if water had washed out the supports under trestles on bridges.

"I invented the device in 1915, but it was 1935 before it was put to use," Mr. Walker said.

Mr. Walker was a con-

ductor for the Southern Pacific for years, two of which was on the Golden State Limited. He also worked on the Cloudcroft line which hauled mostly lumber, and was abandoned when it became cheaper to haul by truck.

"IT WAS A beautiful ride," he said.

The flood detector is arranged so that water raises a float which in turn sets red lights in both directions along the track, warning the engineer, who can bring the train to a halt. It will handle a 200-car train going 70 miles an hour.

The detector must be hand set after it is triggered.

PICTURE: L.R. Walker -- He is a cousin to the Walker boys (Joe, Leck, Glee, Roy and Nat). Lytle R. Walker is a son of Joseph Walker who was a brother to Grandpa Lawrence C. Walker. Lytle's one sister who I wrote to was Fairy Lane who lived in Wichita.

Grandpa Walker (Lawrence C.) named his son Joseph (Joe) after his brother.

8

WALKER MOUNTAIN QUAY COUNTY NEW MEXICO STATE HWY 209

Boyhood Memories 1906

How are things at Walker Mountain?
Is the wind still blowing there?
Do the pinions and the cedars
Crown the mountains everywhere

Do the quail still run like soldiers?
And the coyotes howl at night?
Does the breeze come in from nowhere
Fresh and cold before daylight?

Does the Bermuda grass wave gently
In the southwest summer breeze?
Between the white topped yuccas
And the thorny mesquite trees?

Do the beautiful cactus blossoms
Still look fresh waxed and new
And each thorn on cloudy mornings
Hold one drop of sparkling dew?

I have traveled the world over
By air and land and sea
But still the place I love the best
Is in my boyhood memory.

The Answer to My Boyhood Memories of 1906

All is well at Walker Mountain
The wind is still blowing there.
The green pinions and the cedars
Crown the mountains everywhere.

The quail still run like soldiers
And the coyotes howl at night.
A breeze comes in from nowhere
Fresh and cold before daylight.

The Bermuda grass waves gently
In the southwest summer breeze
Between the white topped yuccas
And the thorny mesquite trees.

I am weary from my travels now
By air and land and sea
I want to rest at Walker Mountain
That is heaven enough for me.

Lawrence Ezra Walker wrote first poem in1975 and published it March 1, 1976 in the El Paso News. A few years before before he passed, he visited Walker Mountain with his daughter June Walker Hollenshead. They found the cave of Walker Mountain and located his initials LEW still on the cave wall written many decades ago. The cave secrets many Walker stories. One tale shared in *Boys Searching for Melons* is that Lawrence Ezra's uncle Lawrence Christler of Sedan, Kansas sheltered his family in the cave until a dugout house could be built. The Walker family is pursuing the proper naming and placing of a monument on Walker Mountain which stands without a name today in the Quay County governmental documents.

9

Benela school house ten
miles S.W. of Tucumcari
New Mexico
Miss Evalina Walker teacher
Pupils were
Emory Walker
- Glen Holt
- Ilene Walker
Lynne Walker
Hugh Moore

Katy Dyer
Ted Dyer
Lela Belle Moore
Rosie May Moore
Jack Briscoe

About 1908
near Tucumcari, NM 10

Mabel Maxwell, Latin and Eighth Grade, salary $70.

Doris M. Butt, Domestic Science and Piano, salary $80.

Mae Luttrell, Seventh Grade, salary $65.

Nellie Hershberger, Fifth and Seventh Grades, salary $70.

Anga Elder, Sixth Grade, salary $65.

Evalina Walker, Fifth Grade, salary $60.

Claudia Whittle, Fourth Grade, salary $60.

]\Tary Fitzgerald, First Grade, salary $70.

Lillian A. Bess, Third and Fourth Grades, salary $80.

Cornelia Burke, Second Grade, salary $70.

Eugenia Roy. Third Grade, salary $70.

Willie Lawing, Second Grade, salary $65.

Clara Gerhardt, First Grade, salary $70.

Louise Murphy, Second and Third Gradea, salary $65.

Grace Jeffrey, First Grade, salary $70.

Mabel W. Clark, Kindergarten, salary $100.

BERNALILLO COUNTY.

(A. Montoya, Albuquerque, County Superintendent.)

1. S. M. Smith, Albuquerque, 2n(i, $55, 9 mos.; Moises Saavedra, (915 S. 2nd, Albuquerque).

Josephine V. Creek, Albuquerque, 1st, $55, 9 mos.
Lucy E. Ortiz, Albuquerque, 2nd, $50, 9 mos.
Maria Espinosa, Albuquerque, 1st, $55, 9 mos.
Vicenta Montoya, Albuquerque, 3rd, $50, 9 mos.

2. Lorena Wells, Albuquerque, 2nd, $50, 9 mos.; Juan Griego y Lucero, (Old Albuquerque).

3. Mary S. Rowland, Alameda, Prof. $60, 9 mos.; Abel Lucero y Gurule, (Alameda, N. M.).

Josefita Quintana, Alameda, 1st., $50, 9 mos.
Margaret Schmidt, Albuquerque (724 S. Broadway), Prof., $50, 9 mos.

4. Mrs. J. T. Ortega, Albuquerque, 2nd, $50, 9 mos.; Jose Martinez, (Alameda).

5. Ruth Goss, Albuquerque, 2nd, $65, 9 mos.; J. M. Sanchez, (1322 S. 3rd, Albuquerque).

Erna Schroeder, Albuquerque, 1st, $65, 9 mos.
Selma J. Anderson, Albuquerque, 1st, $60.

6. Estella C. Kelly, 2nd, $65, 9 mos.; Patrocinio Chavez.
Jose J. Lopez, Padillas, Prof., $55, 9 mos.

7. Babarita Chavez, Albuquerque, 3rd, $50, 9 mos.; Juan Olguin, (Albuquerque).

8. Mabel Barton, Albuquerque, 1st, $50, 9 mos.; Pablo Apodaca (Old Albuquerque).

9. Mrs. Maggie Woodworth, 1st, $50, 9 mos.; Jake S. Armijo.
Mrs. Laura Boushka, Armijo, 2nd, $50, 9 mos.

10. P. C. Mora, Escobosa, Per., $50, 7 mos.; Reyes Mora (Chilili).

These students appeared in Plaza Larga School in 1931–32. (Courtesy of Sue Smith Moore)

Right: The Ben Dunlap family gathered in front of their home near Quay to have their picture taken. (Museum Collection)

the name and asked President Woodrow Wilson to name the new post office Woodrow. She was granted that permission. The post office closed in 1916.

Mesa Redondo School was a two-story rock and lumber structure built in 1906 northwest of the big mesa and about a mile east of the Stallard Ranch. Students sat at varnished desks and were taught by such teachers as Mae Dietzman and Sophia Stallard. That school closed in 1920.

Walker School, named for the J. A. Walker family, was built circa 1906. The mountain just west of the Ira Parker home on Highway 209 became known as Walker Mountain. The school was built on the east side of the mountain and was the seat of education for all the Walker children as well as for Farley Stallard. Anna Stephenson, who became Mrs. Tom Horton, and Blanche Swift, who became Mrs. Harve Wallis, were among the teachers.

Bonita School, a mile northwest of Walker Mountain, came into being before statehood. Jack Briscoe, the Dyers, Taylors, and Moores attended it. Alice Briscoe Holt, Rose Nelson, and Evalina Walker were among the teachers. The Briscoes were among the earliest settlers in the area, arriving in the late 1800s.

Emory C. Walker, Jr.

13

Veterans' Memoirs

Back to "Memoirs" Index page

Emory Walker

Denver, Colorado
Korean War Veteran of the United States Army

"Following are some of my memories of my time involved with OP Harry during those critical days. This was written some time ago as part of an autobiography for my daughters.

- Emory Walker

Emory Walker
(Click the picture for a larger view)

OPHSA (Out Post Harry) Memories...

I reported to the army and was sworn in on January 5, 1951. After processing in San Antonio I was sent to the Atlanta General Depot in Atlanta, Georgia. There I spent six weeks of Signal Corps basic training in the 579th Signal Depot Company. That was a laugh - I had learned more about army basics in high school ROTC than there. Anyway, when that stint was finished My CO called me in to see what signal corps school I wanted to attend since I had qualified for anything the army offered in that vein. I told him that I had been accepted for OCS but had not yet received my orders. He placed me in a radar repair school in Ft. Monmouth, New Jersey but the OCS orders caught up with me before Leaving for New Jersey. I did manage a three day pass tacked onto a weekend and got a hop courtesy of the Air Force to Dallas and a bus ride to El Paso. The objective was to get my car and drive back to Atlanta which I did. My next assignment was to Fort Jackson, South Carolina for Infantry Leadership Training School. Because I had not been in Infantry basic training I was assigned to a basic training company in the 28th Infantry, 8th Infantry Division.

My time in the 28th Infantry was in a trainee capacity for a week or two after which I was transferred to another regiment as cadre. One night I was the CQ (Charge of Quarters) and I was looking through various stuff in the office. I ran across the name of an old friend, Oscar T. Buchholz (who had been a member of St. Mark's Methodist Church in El Paso and had worked for MST & T Co. when I was a frameman). He was listed as the Field Officer of the Day. I called him and he asked where I was. I told him and he came over to my company. It was really funny, before Buck arrived my company commander, a 2nd Lt. came into the office. When Buck arrived with his gold leaves and the

Out Post Harry
Photo taken by James Jarboe
June 15, 1953
(Click picture for a larger view)

FOD arm band my CO about died. Buck said he didn't want to see the Lt. but had come to visit Emory instead. We saw quite a lot of each other while at Ft. Jackson and I often went to their house for dinner after church. Buck had been recalled after service during World War II. A little more about him later.

When I reported to the Leadership Training School I was really surprised to find my friend, Buck, was the commanding officer. Upon completion of that school there was an automatic promotion to corporal involved so I never was a PFC. When my orders for OCS arrived it included an automatic promotion to staff sergeant so I was a very short term corporal. I remember the first sergeant of whatever company I was in at the time couldn't understand how someone could be promoted so fast after so short a time in the army. I reported to Fort Benning, Georgia in October of 1952 as a member of OC Class 11A.*

Until graduation day on April 21, 1952, I had experiences like I could not imagine. Because of how tall I was I was assigned to the first platoon. Too bad! The platoon leader and tactical Officer was a 2nd Lt. William H. Tyler, an

Sunset On A War
Photo taken by James Jarboe
July 27, 1953
(Click picture for a larger view)

SOB if ever one lived. He had just graduated from the Citadel that spring and had just completed his advanced infantry class at Ft. Benning. He knew all of the ways to make officer candidates eat dirt, and he did. He was probably the most despised individual among the company because he took sadistic delight in harassing every member of the company regardless of which platoon the individual was in.

Fairly early in our tenure in OC Class 11A the company commander put together a team to write and edit a class yearbook of sorts. I was very fortunate to be named the photographer for that effort. I requested permission to do all of the processing, printing, etc. of all the photographs and he agreed. This meant that I had to have a class A pass to get off the post where we were stationed to go to the main post photo lab to do the work. What a deal! OCS with a class A pass. The class book staff had a special room assigned to it which was never to be inspected by order of the commanding officer. That proved to be heaven. Bob Andrews was the editor (and we were room mates for quite a while) and had an affinity for bourbon having been an INS reporter in Dallas prior to the army.

Having a car and a class A pass proved to be a real benefit. I could make a run to the main post, do some photography work and swing by a nearby package liquor store. Of course, those bottles stayed in that never inspected room. Working on that class book was a real opportunity to meet and get to know everyone in the company. We had decided early on that our class book would be individualized rather than like some of the boiler plate stuff others had done. One thing this meant was a candid photo of every member of the class to appear along side his graduation picture. I still have my copy of the book and really cherish it.

14

The experiences of those six months in OCS are far too numerous to mention here but a few highlights will have to suffice. The fall of 1952 was mostly spent in the basics of map reading, tactics, marksmanship, etc. The only remarkable thing was that I was top in the class with the M1 rifle, the carbine and the BAR having made the highest qualifying scores. With the .45 pistol I was lucky if I could hit the ground. I did respectfully well with the other weapons, light and heavy machine guns, mortars (60 mm, 81 mm and 4.2"), and even artillery. When Christmas time rolled around there was a question of whether we could go home or not. The decision was finally a YES. What a welcome break to some very serious tension. I managed to get back to El Paso via an air force hop and returned to Ft. Benning via train.

We had to report in no later than midnight on January 1, 1952. I remember I arrived in town that afternoon and fooled around until evening when I got back to the company. It took Lt. Tyler no time at all to begin the harassing again, even before we had to report back. We finally got to bed after midnight and to some very welcome sleep. I think it was about 4:00 or 4:30 in the morning when we were all aroused to be greeted with a major obstacle. It was customary to begin each day with calisthenics but this day was to be special. Double timing was common and running was not out of the question. This day, however, was both. At our early morning formation we were told we were going on a fourteen mile excursion. For the first seven miles we double timed and stopped for about a fifteen minute break. We then double timed for two or three miles on the way back but were stopped and told we would run the rest of the way. Anyone who failed to return with the rest of the company would be automatically expelled from OCS. We lost about one third of the class left at that time. (Several had been expelled for various reasons during the first three months.)

It wasn't too long after surviving that awful January 2nd that all of a sudden we were slated for an inspection by none less than General Mark Clark, Chief of Staff of the U S Army. What an honor? It seemed necessary to our Tac Officers that the company area needed some sprucing up and a new coat of paint. Of course, that was the order of the day (I really should say nights because that is when all the work was done) except we had no paint. That meant we "contributed" some of our meager pay with which to buy paint. Needless to say, that company area was a knockout when General Clark arrived. In fact, he was quite impressed. Somehow after that episode we managed to get a few coveted, weekend passes.

One of the things stressed during OCS was physical fitness. Every morning we did calisthenics and a lot of double-timing, running, etc. We had a couple of practice physical fitness tests on which I was only about average. Then came the three tests which were for the record. Those were really stressful but I managed to ace them. It seems that on the Saturday morning of our first record test I had two wisdom teeth pulled. It was pretty obvious, even to Lt. Tyler, that there was no way I could do very well on that test. When the second record test day arrived, another Saturday, guess what? I had the two remaining wisdom teeth pulled. Even with that I did manage to show some improvement over the first test so that was good. Improvement was the main goal. When the final test arrived I was near the top of the class in improvement because I had no more wisdom teeth to come out.

One of the evaluation techniques was to send candidates before an officer evaluation board. This was a dreaded experience because that board could summarily kick one out of OCS, send him back to another company or pass him along to continue with the class. My board experience was a real trying time. It seemed that most, if not all, of our platoon were sent before the board for any reason Lt. Tyler could dream up. I managed to survive and did graduate with my class. From that point on my one big goal in the army was to outrank Lt. Tyler, and I almost made it. More on that later.

April 21, 1952 was a BIG day. What was left of OC Class 11A were brand new 2nd Lieutenants, absolutely the lowest form of life in all of the army. That probably goes for the Marines and Air Force, too. Several of my class mates stayed on at Ft. Benning to attend parachute school. At that time I wanted nothing more to do with Ft. Benning so did not volunteer for that training. That is probably the biggest regret I have concerning my five years in the army - not learning to jump out of airplanes. I have regretted that decision ever since.

I was assigned to Ft. Leonard Wood, Missouri to the 94th Infantry Battalion (Separate) as a platoon leader. This was an interesting and good experience for a brand new 2nd Lt. This unit was one of the last segregated units in the army with all black troops and about two-thirds white officers. The reason that training was so good was that everything that could happen did happen in that unit. We always had the best of everything on the post - best day room, best mess hall, best supply room, etc. On the other hand every problem that could come up in the army probably happened there. We had AWOL as a matter of course, summary courts martial of all kinds, many crimes both on and off post, general courts martial, and more company punishment that one could imagine. They were either very good or just terrible.

One of the nice side benefits of being assigned to this unit was the battalion commander. It seems he had a girl friend in Kansas City and wanted to spend the weekends with her. As a result he would always arrange for a night training exercise during the week and give everyone Saturday morning as compensatory time off. That was just great. Some of us from the BOQ had gotten acquainted with the Haggadorns who owned a lodge, or resort, on the Lake of the Ozarks. Bill Haggadorn had a problem in that the lodge had a great many single girls from Kansas City and St. Louis who would spend a week or two at the lake. Bill's problem was a shortage of young men for these girls to square dance with or whatever kind of dancing was to go on at the time. He also needed young men to escort these women on some of the hayrack rides, etc. So naturally, he encouraged us to spend our free time at the lake and to further encourage us he gave us everything at half price. Not a bad deal. I did meet some very nice girls this way but nothing developed in a very serious vein. It was during this period that I received my one and only proposal of marriage. Some girl thought I was what she wanted in a husband. I do not even remember her name or what she looked like. I guess it made only a small impression on me.

Another benefit of being stationed in the 94th Infantry Battalion (Separate) was that I got to go to Alaska. One of the platoon leaders had volunteered for Summer Arctic Indoctrination Training but was involved in an auto accident and could not go. At the last minute I volunteered to take his place and was soon on orders to proceed to Great Falls, Montana to connect with a flight to Alaska. In those days the train was the way to get around so I was off to Montana via Denver (the first time I remember ever being in Denver and then only to see the city from a train). I remember when we got to Billings, Montana they set the Pullman car on a side track and said we were welcome to sleep there for the night, a Saturday, as I remember. I know I left the train to wander around Billings and to have dinner somewhere. I was really shaken to see vast numbers of drunk Indians laying on the sidewalks, passed out. We were off to Great Falls early the next morning to meet our flight on Monday.

The trip on an air force C-54 was uneventful. We did stop in Edmonton, Alberta, Canada for refueling before proceeding to Big Delta, Alaska. The arctic indoctrination school was located in Big Delta which is about 90 miles or so south of Fairbanks. As I recall the first couple of weeks was spent teaching us technical climbing, that is using ropes, pitons, etc. This was really a blast because I had always done quite a bit of climbing in younger days.

We then had a weekend on TDY (temporary duty) to Fairbanks so we could see the sights. Two things really impressed me. First was the museum at the University of Alaska where an enormous Kodiak Bear, stuffed and standing on his hind legs, greeted one as he entered the building. That bear must have been at least fourteen

ase commander at Big Delta to see if he needed any instructors

in his staff. He told me to make a formal application for transfer to Big Delt
equest a new 2nd Lt. instructor and name me as the one he wanted. Good l(

ome things I particularly remember about my Alaskan experience was learn
xtremes. Near where I was, the record low and record high both occurred. I
ecord high was a bit over 100 degrees while the low recorded was around 9(
laska being so far north it is truly the land of the midnight sun. I remember
ome time around eleven o'clock and finding the sun still brightly shining. I r
elta the sun was coming up and it was around three-thirty in the morning. I
ight that was. We were in a C-54, not too bad an airplane, and ran into a fe
ocky Mountains. That plane rode like a bucking bronco and everyone aboar
nd crew. It was awful.

.t that time any request for a transfer involving a change of station required
holces. My first was Big Delta, the second Europe and the third was for FEC(
ranslated to Korea). Guess which one I got.

lpon returning to Ft. Leonard Wood just in time for the Labor Day weekend
o go back to Alaska. One of the things I had to do was set up some training
lad learned in Alaska. We did some minor technical rope work and I taught 1
ireat fun.

'raining was a very big thing and my favorite class to instruct at that time w
layonet. When one learns how to do it the danger of being stabbed is absolt
his very well and did a lot of teaching. I remember one day one of the GI's
n his training and the attention he was not giving to me, the know-it-all 2nd
xercise properly so I started picking on him until he was really getting mad
)ut he didn't know it. Finally, I told him to stab me with his bayonet which w
:new if he really tried I was kidding him. As it turned out I kept nagging him until he
ull intention of killing me. He didn't. I easily disarmed him and in doing so a
he butt of his rifle and broke a couple of his ribs. From that moment on tho:
)aying attention when I was the instructor.

3y this time things were all over between Anne Marsh and me so when I got
Korea I managed to date a couple of other girls. One I remember was Barba
ligh school. I remember taking her to an affair at the Ft. Bliss Officer's Club
lad known before in the army. I cannot remember who we met but I do rer
:ouple of times. She was one of the girls I also knew at Trinity Methodist Ch

: had to leave El Paso in early December to go to Ft. Lawton, Washington fo
almost three weeks before we sailed which was a surprise to me. Usually th(
:here was such a turnover and replacements were in short supply. But the U
of travel. We sailed on the worst possible date, December 24, 1952. I doubt
ike to set sail on Christmas Eve. But sail we did! The people of Seattle had
;ervicemen home from Korea when a troop ship arrived. This was the excep
:here were many protests about the Korean "Police Action." Anyway, on this
:rue. People turned out in droves to wish us well and give out over four thot
;end off!

With the holiday season at hand one might well imagine there was more tha
refreshments on board that troop ship. It was well hidden until someone ca(
bottle. That did it and the booze flowed from that time onward. The trip wa:
a major northern Pacific storm which lasted for three weeks. The captain of
storm but to no avail. We went south to just north of the Hawaiian Islands &
Philippines Sea to get to Japan. I was one who got seasick going to Catalina
me. Since I was one of the few not seasick I was made the mess officer. No
ill troops. We did spend quite a bit of time playing Canasta, cribbage and a l
eventually made it to Japan none the worse for all the travails of that crossi
Yokohama and Mount Fuji and some seas without 30 foot waves.

Aboard ship, one of my roommates turned out to be quite a valuable acqua
very senior officer of a New York bank which had a branch office in Tokyo. V
he contacted the branch manager who in turn furnished him with a car and
Camp Drake was a replacement center and we were required to report in tv
had orders. The rest of the time was ours. With the availability of the car ar
Tokyo, Yokahama and as far south as Kokura (sp?), and we really took adv:
seeing was missed. It is hard for me to realize just how fortunate I have be
another example.

Towards the end of January I was assigned to Korea but with no specific as:
had left the states Buck Buchholz had told me to look him up when I got to
Camp Drake. He was then assigned to the POW camp on Koji-Do (sp?), I th
then he was a Lt. Colonel.) Anyway, Buck asked me if I would like to be as:
declined and said I wanted to take my chances elsewhere, and besides, I tc

16

Officer in OCS. That was the last time I ever talked to Buck; we completely lost track of each other and have never reestablished a link since.

Again, instead of flying to Korea I went via MSTS, this time the USS Marine Lynx. It was only an overnight trip so not much happened on that short crossing of the Sea of Japan to Korea. The pipeline, the vehicle for processing replacement personnel, soon had me assigned to the Third Infantry Division. This was and still is an old and very proud division with an impeccable record from both World Wars I and II. My assignment then was to the 15th Infantry Regiment, another old and proud unit with a distinguished record for a great many years with the motto "Can Do". This motto came from the 15th's days in China during the later part of the 1800's. The 15th Infantry was commanded by Colonel Richard Stilwell (he retired as a four star general) who briefly greeted the new arrivals upon reaching the his HQ. I was assigned to the 2nd Battalion of the 15th as a Platoon Leader of the 3rd platoon of Company F.

The 2nd Battalion consisted of companies E, F, G, H, and HQ and was commanded by Major John K. Singlaub (who ended his army career as a two star general). My company commander was Captain Kless von Guysen and the other platoon leaders were John Mitchell, Jim Baker and ????. The Executive Officer was ????. Our company was located on a part of the MLR (main line of resistance) immediately behind Outpost Harry. Our regimental sector had responsibility for Outposts Tom, Dick and Harry. Tom was located on the edge of the Chorwan valley while Dick was just to the east. Harry was a company size outpost but at the time I joined Company F we had only a reinforced platoon there.

My first days of combat resulted in nothing happening except for lots of patrols. My platoon would get a patrol assignment about every fourth night or so and were of the ambush type of patrol. We were not to look for trouble but rather be a point of first contact with the Chinese if they were to launch anything. At some point my platoon rotated out to Outpost Harry for a stay of a few days. Those episodes were pretty routine except that occasionally the Chinese would lob a mortar round or two just to keep us on our toes. I never really heard a shot fired in anger except for the friendly artillery that was fairly constant. My days as a platoon leader were days devoted to developing strong friendships with my fellow officers and the men in my platoon."

When I took over the 3rd platoon I was warned that I would have a difficult time replacing Lt. Hutchinson, a West Pointer who was adored by the men. Fortunately, for me, that was never a problem. When I was at Ft. Leonard Wood my company commander had just returned from Korea. When I asked him for advice he gave me two pieces - take along a one burner gasoline stove and a large coffee pot. This I did and was that ever good advice! My platoon sergeant was about to rotate back to the states and was worthless as a platoon sergeant so I gave him one order, the coffee pot was to be full at all times. This was especially true after a patrol because the patrol members were mighty glad to have hot coffee when they came in from freezing their butts. This gesture really endeared those men to me.

During the long nights when we had a patrol out everyone was on a 100% alert and often when there was no patrol. During some of these times John Mitchell undertook to write a poem about our experiences. That poem follows:

Korea - early 1953

Tired, cold, scared - The fear obvious in their steps and eyes.

Men, maybe; boys mostly -
    The boy from Michigan who skis
    The boy from Brooklyn who wants to fight but is scared to death
    - - - talk only-

This one loads and reloads a thirty round clip, curved to be held.
"When I get back to Virginia, man, all I want is a girl and my bakery truck."

Here's one - Calm, steely eyes -
    He hates patrols, his guts twist inside him -
    two-seven-zero Jackson Heights Chorwon -

"Yea, I'm ready" - "Everybody got grenades?" "Yes, Lieutenant"
    Another Lieutenant - the seventh, no, sixth, - - they move so fast -
    Fourth Platoon, Battalion, Rotation, (yea, Quartermaster Rotation).

Dig all day - - Patrol all night
    Dig Patrol Dig Patrol Dig - Just five more points.

There stands the Lieutenant, new Lieutenant,
    Shiny (no, not shiny now, serious; scared too; doesn't show it
    much, though) sort of a nice guy - - likes to laugh -
    No brass on the collar now, no green-gold bar - Just like a G-I;
    almost.

Password - - Mae West Call Sign - - Suffering Succotash
    Pyrotechnics: Green Star - Amber Parachute - Red Star cluster

Check Points - Obvious
    Anxious
    and, Damn - - can't remember -

"Joe Chink's not going to get Coco!" -
"Not tonight or ever, Coco - - we go out as a unit - come back as a unit - "Yea"

"O.K., Let's go. -

Jose (doesn't speak much English, but sure can fire that AR) crosses
    himself - Quiet, confident, a good soldier, R.A.

Black, Dark, Night, Deep, - Deep, Dark, Black, Night.

Safe Lane, damn, be quiet.
    Barbed wire Barbed wire
    Barbed wire Concertina
    Concertina Barbed wire Barbed wire

Point man moves - stops - listens - looks - Patrol moves -
There it is! Artillery moonbeam - There! Now we can see -

Cross the creek, up the path -
   "Wire, commo wire - must be a million miles of the stuff in this
   damned safe lane."

Step easy -- Walk slow
--Bet we sound like a Battalion to the Chinks - -

Quad fifty cracks overhead - Deadly Christmas Tree Lights
Red, rosy, friendly - Red, angry, tearing

Slow, move, stop, move -
Ambush site up ahead (ours or theirs?)
Eyes and ears strain - damn those people -
Who? Everybody in this stinking country.

KATUSA (small Korean, can't pronounce his name - Mim Jung Ki or
   something.) Moves out behind the commo-man (boy from Michigan
   (likes to ski).

STOP

The lieutenant moves out into the darkness, two men cover him as he
   moves - Hope we're here first.

THE CHINESE SOLDIER IS WELL TRAINED, WELL EQUIPPED AND CRAFTY

   Move, the troops are watching -

"Fool! - just five more points - no more patrols - just dig - more
   sukoshi - HOME -

Don't like this place - just like Two-seven-zero - Jackson Heights -
   Chorwon

Damn Lieutenant doesn't know how -- good ambush site though.

Cold, wet, cold, cold, cold, cold - Mickey Mouse boots, number one
   Hands cold, feet warm - Mickey Mouse gloves, havano!

--Wake up that damned medic - Chinese can hear him snore across the
   valley -

Sleep, warm, comfortable - Cold, wet, cold, cold, cold. Sit here,
   wait, freeze, sit.

The tank fires, splitting the air, everyone jumps.

Come back - maybe -

Time - slow, cold time, short, fast sleep - long cold wait.

Move out - No chinks tonight - Quiet - God Damn - Quiet -

Wake up everybody -

Slowly - - not so fast - - easy. Down the path - Cross the creek -
Into the safe lane and now - -

HALT

The bolt goes back. Snaps forward
   Mr. Browning's machine gun is now fully loaded -

Voices - - Dark -

Mae - - - - an AR bolt goes back in the patrol - - - - West.

O.K.

Move in - count noses - back to the platoon - Tell the old man, - - go
   to bed, - Bed! Sleep!

No more for a couple of nights - -

Damn - - just gotta get five more points -

      by Lt. John A. Mitchell; Co. F, 15th Inf.

I remember only one specific patrol with any clarity. Most were simply ambush patrols but one was special. It was what was known as a combat patrol. This meant we went out specifically to try to find and engage the Chinese. Before the patrol was to go out I requested an aerial reconnaissance of the area we were going to cover. This was done in an L-19 airplane, a small two seater. I remember the pilot must have been married with several kids because he had no thought of going low enough for me to see anything.

Eventually I convinced the pilot the Chinese slept during the day and he should make one pass down the valley we were going into so I could see. We made that pass to the east of Outpost Harry and right down the adjoining valley. Just as we crossed the Chinese MLR they opened up with a machine gun and managed to stitch a few holes in our tail. No damage done and there were no injuries. When we came roaring down that valley we crossed immediately over the position of my platoon. My troops had my Texas flag out on the top of my bunker and we couldn't miss seeing it. That flag was a gift from the Mitchell Brewing Co. in El Paso, something they did for anyone going to Korea.

When we got back to the airstrip I returned to my regimental headquarters and greeting me there was an Episcopal chaplain, Major Marsh. He told me he understood what I was about to embark on and offered a prayer for our safe return. It worked!

Another interesting patrol involved taking a 2nd Lt. from the division G-2 along with a war dog. These were dogs trained to warn the handler of a potential problem. That dog really saved us by alerting us of a Chinese patrol across a small valley. We were able to call in some mortar fire on them and they dispersed. Since that was right in front of the Greek position they sent out a patrol to mop up.

I so remember coming in from one of the early patrols I took out and having a real problem. When we came in we had to cross through a safe lane and clear our weapons. This night was bitterly cold and it had snowed. When we started to clear our weapons we found all the bolts were frozen closed. Had we run into any Chinese that night we could each have fired only one round. Even the pins on our hand grenades were frozen in and could not be readily pulled.

My platoon position was the right flank of the entire 3rd Division tied in with the Greek unit on my right. Infantry training always teaches that where two diverse units are joined at a point, that is a source of real weakness because of communications, etc. Because of this the Assistant Division Commander, Brigadier General Dunkleburg, spent a lot of time in my area making sure that all was well. Over a few weeks I became well acquainted with the general and he with me. It was probably sometime in about March when I received the finest compliment of my army career. General Dunkleburg told Major Singlaub and Captain Guysen that mine was the best platoon in the entire 3rd Division. Talk about brownie points, that really did it!

It wasn't long after that that I was transferred to Company H as the Recon Officer. General Smyth, the 3rd Division Commanding General had decided we needed to fortify a mountain immediately behind the Greek positions and my job was to direct the Greeks in doing this. I was assigned an interpreter, Lt. Vakalopoulos, who proved to be a very fine gentleman and friend. He was about as tough an officer as I had ever known. One night the Greeks were involved in a pretty serious fire fight with the Chinese while both were on patrols. One of the Greeks killed that night was a Lieutenant who was a boyhood friend of Lt. Vakalopoulos and the two of them had served together in the Greek army for some time. I expressed my sorrow to my interpreter who was pretty philosophical about his friend's death. He said this is war and these things must be expected. Army friendships are not easy!

An interesting sidelight about my time in H company was quite a bit of poker playing. Captain Rizzo, Lt. Huddleston and some of the platoon leaders plus some officers from the 5th RCT joined us on occasion. When ever there was no alert we could play and that happened fairly often during that time. I was incredibly lucky with my playing and one night I had held a few pat hands and won the pot. Everyone was getting a little more than exasperated at my luck. In one hand late in the game I was dealt three aces and the joker plus a garbage card. Since I had won so many hands with a pat hand I discarded the garbage card and drew the other ace. Needless-to-say, I simply laid down my hand and won the pot, again. Great fun! I won enough during those days to make a $500.00 down payment on a car later.

It was during my time with company H that Outpost Harry was hit with a small Chinese probe. Company F had the responsibility for the outpost on that night and Jim Baker was the platoon leader. They were able to drive the Chinese off the outpost and Jim distinguished himself in a true John Wayne style, shooting a light machine gun from the hip. For his bravery and daring that night Jim received the Distinguished Service Cross, the second highest decoration for valor. Jim and I have kept in contact with each other these many years via Christmas cards and a visit with each other a couple of times. He remained in the Army Reserves and eventually retired as a Brigadier General.

While working with the Greeks I received a call from the 2nd Battalion Adjutant telling me to report to Battalion HQ. Of course I did just that as fast as my little old jeep would permit. When I got there I was almost ignored. Major Singlaub made some small talk and we had a cigarette or two along with coffee. Eventually, a cloud of dust approached and out of it came General Dunkleburg who together with major Singlaub pinned the silver bars of a 1st Lieutenant on my collar. Boy was I one surprised GI. When I got back with the Greeks my interpreter noticed the promotion and that called for a party.

*It seems that in the Greek army a promotion is almost unheard of, one must do something special to rate one. The Greeks had a great advantage over the American troops in that they were allowed to have liquor on the line. That party is where I was first introduced to Greek liquors, both Metaxa and Ouso. I still like Metaxa to this day and enjoy it once in a while. I remember that the Greeks had some of the finest bread one could ever eat. I do not know how they obtained the ingredients and raw materials, but they really did eat well. So did I at that party.

Colonel Stilwell had been reassigned and was replaced by a Colonel Russell Akers. Colonel Stilwell (no relation to general Vinegar Joe Stilwell) was such a fine officer it was a shame to have him leave. His replacement was Colonel Russell Akers who was an alcoholic. Col. Akers was not one to leave his regimental headquarters but rather to stay in that relatively safe environment. It seems that it might have been in May when there was another fire fight on Outpost Harry. Major Singlaub was always a hands on type of commander and during this engagement he was very busy organizing a relief of Harry. Col. Akers called him to ask what was going on and the good major didn't have time to talk to him. Major Frank Hewitt, the battalion executive officer told Col. Akers that the battalion CO didn't have time to talk to him so Col Akers relieved Major Singlaub on the spot. Interestingly, it was only a few weeks after this unfortunate incident that it became Lt. Col. Singlaub.

It was during my stint in Company H that I found out where the hated Lt. Tyler was stationed. I called him and learned he had beat me to 1st Lt. by only a few weeks. It seems he spent the normal 18 months as a 2nd Lt. while my promotion came in a year and nine days. I also learned that his time in Korea was as a platoon leader only so I think I really outdid him.

It was in late May that Col. Akers got a bee in his rum soaked brain that I should be on his staff as an Assistant S-3 and had orders cut to that effect. I was livid to think I would be stuck in some HQ with an alcoholic CO so I called General Dunkleburg to see if anything could be done about the orders. My overwhelming desire was to outrank Lt. Tyler. At that time a company commander who was a 1st Lt. could be promoted to Captain after ninety days so that was my route! (The general had told me to call him if I ever needed anything, so I did.) A day or two later the orders were rescinded and replaced with orders naming me as company commander of Company G which had just come off line into a regimental reserve area.

Captain Atkinson had been the CO of Company G and had been relieved along with his 1st Sergeant. I never did learn what they did but the good thing was that I had become a company commander. This was in the period in the army where companies had a Warrant Officer as a Unit Administrator. Mine was a WOJG Jug Black who was an old timer in the army. I told Jug his first job was to find us a First Sergeant and suggested he scour the regiment for someone who had been a Master Sergeant for awhile and who would like a crack at being "first soldier." Jug found someone who fit the requirements and I had him transferred to Company G. Company G was really in a shambles with poor morale, little discipline and in need of a lot of work. One of my first moves was to fire the Exec officer, the supply sergeant and the mess sergeant. It was simply intolerable for me to have such incompetents around.

19

Company G had been pulled into a regimental reserve area where we did some small amount of training and started to get reorganized. This is when I learned the true value of a scrounger. WOJG Jug Black was a scrounger of the first order and could really get things done. We were very short of the thirty round magazines for carbine rifles so I asked Jug if he could get us some. He asked what I had to trade and said some kind of souvenir would be best. I did have a cap from a dead Chinese soldier which still had its small red star on it so I gave that to Jug and he was off. A couple of hours later he returned with as many magazines as could be loaded into a jeep.

Being in a reserve area electricity would be nice so again I asked Jug what he could do about a generator. Again the question about trading material came up and this time it would take something pretty good. We had just received our class VI ration so I had some liquor and could use that. I gave him a couple bottles of scotch and away he went. When he got back he did indeed have a generator behind a 2 1/2 ton truck, and a trailer to move it with, and gasoline, and electric wire and whatever else two bottles of scotch could obtain. We did have electricity!

We had the new generator only a day or two when the battalion commander came through the company area on an inspection trip. When he saw that generator he just about flipped. He wanted to know where I had gotten it, etc. I told him and he said that I didn't even have a vehicle capable of moving it and I agreed. He said he had a small generator which could easily supply my company while my generator could supply the entire battalion headquarters and, he could move it, so we traded. We were both happy with that deal!

During this time I developed an intense hatred for the Red Cross and whatever it stood for. It seems that one of the sergeants in the company received a letter from his mother telling of a heart attack that his father had. In the letter she said she had contacted the Red Cross to try to arrange an emergency leave for the son. The telegram to the Red Cross representative in our regiment was never delivered to me so I could authorize the emergency leave. A couple days later the sergeant received another letter from his mother saying his father had died and she could not understand why he had not gotten home to see his father. My investigation proved to be incredible. The Red Cross representative was an alcoholic who never bothered to do anything with the telegrams about the sergeants father. Had I gotten the information in time he could have gotten home and seen his father before he died. After a death there was no provision for an emergency leave at that time so he could do nothing. I know a lot of men in that company stopped any contribution to the Red Cross because of that incident. I know that I did.

It was on June 10, 1953 the Chinese launched an all out offensive to take Outpost Harry. General Maxwell Taylor, the commanding general of the Far East Command said this outpost was a hold-at-all-costs position. It seems that Harry occupied such a commanding position that to loose it would have necessitated our MLR being shifted almost seven miles south. With the so-called peace talks going on at the time that was not a good idea. Company K received the initial assault by about 3,600 Chinese. The company held but suffered almost 100% KIA and WIA. Captain Martin Markley was the CO and I later met him for the first time at Fitzsimmons Army Hospital.

On June 11th the Chinese launched a rare daylight attack with about a battalion size attack but were soon repulsed. On the 12th another assault, this time with a Chinese regiment attempted to take Harry but could not. I think it was on the 12th that Company G was ordered into a support position behind Outpost Tom and I had a platoon of tanks attached. That was the first time I had ever had to contend with tanks and fortunately I didn't have to use them.

The 13th Harry was pretty calm with only a company sized attack and then came the 14th. Company G was ordered to Harry under the operational control of one of the battalion commanders of the 5th Regimental Combat Team and I was to return to a once very familiar piece of ground. Wrong! That outpost looked like nothing I could remember. On the way out to Harry we passed by immense piles of Chinese bodies. Climbing up Harry we saw countless pieces of both Chinese and GI's body parts laying all over the place. The trenches were mostly caved in from all of the intense shelling that had been going on. I later learned that the Chinese had fired about 89,000 rounds larger than 81 mm in size to support their attacks while our forces fired over 368,000 similar size rounds. (I understand this amount of large caliber ammunition was more than was fired by both sides during the entire Battle of the Bulge in World War II.)

We spent all the day of the 14th trying to refurbish the trench lines and bunkers which were by then quite devastated. The first thing I did when I got to the top of the once familiar Outpost Harry was to remove all radio antennas. I had learned that the Chinese zeroed in on antennas. One of the smart things I ever did in regard to combat occurred that day. I had my communications team bury four separate land lines for our telephones along the sides of the trench leading back towards the MLR. After the lines were buried I had them buried further and covered with steel pickets used for barbed wire. This meant that we should have decent telephone communications for a while when the Chinese started their TOT. It did indeed work out that way. The other good thing I did that day was something Major Singlaub had preached about - VT on our positions. I arranged defensive artillery and mortar barrages to begin on a timed sequence. Unless ordered to cease fire, the last barrages were to be VT on top of us. I feel very confident that last stage saved G Company from being completely overwhelmed.

In the early evening of the 14th an artillery sergeant from the 39th Field Artillery attached to my company along with a forward observer decided he was going to wage his own private war when the Chinese came. He got up on the top of the CP bunker and built a sandbag emplacement where he said he could fight any Chinese who came that way. As he was nearing the completion of his position the Chinese started shelling with their 61 mm mortars. The sergeant was hit and very badly wounded. His left arm had been blown off. I went to the top of the bunker and managed to get him out of the mortar barrage and back into the relative safety of the trench outside the bunker. He was unconscious and bleeding profusely. We got the battalion surgeon on the phone and he told me what to do to try to save him. I managed to get a tourniquet on the stump of his arm and our medics got him off the outpost and to the battalion aid station. A little later the doctor called me and said in spite of all our efforts he did not make it. For the life of me I cannot remember his name.

This was OP Harry on June 15th when I was wounded. Of course, the outpost is the large hill in the center of the picture.
Photo courtesy of Jim Jarboe, Combat Photographer,
3rd Infantry Division
(Click the picture for a larger view)

Very early on the 15th of June the Chinese started their initial barrage. The incoming mortar and artillery in the volumes they were using is impossible to describe to anyone who has not experienced anything like that. It was devastating. I very foolishly started to make the rounds of my platoon leaders to make sure all men were inside their bunkers when the barrage started. In spite of the trenches for getting around in I was wounded quite severely within just a few minutes. I remember being temporarily deafened by the noise and was crouched down in a trench. My arms were supporting me by holding onto the sides of the trench when I was hit. It was in the left arm and my hand was left attached by only two shreds of skin on either side of my wrist. I never knew for sure what got me but I strongly suspect it might have been a mortar fuse or possibly a hand grenade.

20

I eventually made it to our medic's station which I had placed at the bottom rear of Outpost Harry in what was left of a bunker. The medic was unable to stop the bleeding enough for me to get back to my CP and about the only thing he did was to give me an unwanted shot of morphine which caused me to be unable perform any duty. An armored personnel carrier evacuated several of us to the battalion aid station where Doc Merrifield along with John Mitchell was more than busy. Several ambulances started the trek to the 44th MASH and I was such a bloody mess that chaplains managed to give me last rites on three different occasions before I got to the MASH. (Much later, after reading General Singlaub's book Hazardous Duty, I learned that the 44th MASH was the model for the TV series M*A*S*H 4077) Isn't it interesting what things come to mind when writing something like this?

Previously, during my short army career I had donated blood on five separate occasions. From the time I arrived at the battalion aid station until I left the MASH I had received back six pints. I guess that is why I was such a bloody mess during those first few hours after being wounded. I remember asking a doctor if they were going to amputate my arm. His answer was no, if they could restore circulation to my hand. It seems that was the criteria to amputate or not.

I remember that after the surgery under a general anesthetic at the MASH I had just regained consciousness. There were three generals waiting to talk to me; I think it might have been Lieutenant General Jenkins who asked me how we had managed to maintain telephone communications for such a long time through the Chinese shelling. When I told him he said that was rather an expensive but very effective means. The other generals were Ridings and Dunkelburg.

I was in the MASH for only a day or so and was evacuated to the 121st Evac Hospital where I spent another couple of days waiting transport to Japan. It was from the MASH to the 121st that I had my first and only helicopter ride. I was in one of those carriers attached to the side of the chopper on the landing struts. From the 121st I was sent to the Osaka Army Hospital in Osaka, Japan.

MG Eugene Ridings (3ID Commander) and LTG Rueben Jenkins (Corps Commander) was taken by James Jarboe at Division Headquarters.
(Click picture for a larger view)

While in Osaka the doctors did an operation called a debridement which was a procedure to remove dead and/or infected tissue. They also changed bandages and casts a couple of times and started antibiotics. One thing I particularly remember from Osaka was a typhoon. I have never seen so much or so intense rain before or since. Each drop must have been a quart or so. I know that all of the wounded in the orthopedics ward where I was experienced very severe pain because of the drastic drop in the barometric pressure. As soon as the storm reached us the nurses were on their rounds with shots of morphine.

One really funny thing happened while at Osaka. I had been taken back to my room from recovery and was still quite groggy. My roommate later told me that when I started to come around I was singing The Eyes of Texas and told him to stand at attention when he heard the national anthem. He swore that really happened. Another thing I recall is going to the officers club with a nurse for a dinner. It was kind of strange since I had no uniform, only hospital clothes but they let me in anyway. The only thing I remember about her was she was very nice and was either Amish or a Mennonite and had volunteered for nursing duty in the army.

While at the hospital I was able to complete a call home to tell the folks that I was in pretty good shape. Those telegrams from the War Department are pretty stiff without very much information. I know the call lasted about fifteen minutes and cost three dollars per minute. I said I would call from Hawaii to let them know I was on the way home and they said to call collect.

I had recovered my savings from my poker games from our battalion safe before I left the MASH. I remember John Mitchell was hopping mad because he couldn't bring the money to me at the MASH. Anyway I did get it and used it as a down payment on a new 1953 Plymouth sedan to be picked up in Detroit after I got home. There was some kind of a problem with the person who handled the automobile sales and the CID contacted me about my arrangement. I had made the contact through the hospital so there was no problem there. I know a CID agent took me some place to identify that person which I did. There was no problem for me and I picked up the car later. Apparently, some people had been taken for their down payments and never got their cars. I was very fortunate!

Only a few days were spent in Osaka before starting the trek back to the states via the MATS (Military Air Transport Service). We flew from Osaka to Tokyo to meet up with others to be evacuated back and were at the Tokyo hospital for only a few hours until our flight left. I remember the plane was a C-54 equipped with stretchers all over the place. There were nurses and a doctor on board to look after all of us. The trip, for the most part, was uneventful. Our first stop was on Midway Island for refueling. I was ambulatory and could walk around Midway for a couple of hours. I wish I had had a camera! Watching those Gooney birds (a kind of gull) was hilarious. To take off they would run as fast as their short legs could carry them flapping their wings furiously. Most often they would tumble head over tail and not get airborne. Usually it took a bird several tries to get into the air. Once up they were very graceful but their landing was just the opposite of their takeoff. They would coast down to the ground as graceful as could be but as soon as the touched down they tumbled for several yards getting stopped.

Our next stop was in Honolulu, Hawaii. We landed at the Air Force base there and were taken to Tripler Army Hospital to spend the night. As soon as we landed there was a swarm of Red Cross types with fresh pineapple juice. That had absolutely no appeal to me because it had been months since I had any fresh milk. I asked if such was available and it was. I cannot remember anything tasting so good as that glass of cold, fresh milk. The other thing I particularly remember about Tripler was waking up the next morning. My room was loaded with fresh flowers.

Eventually I arrived at Fitzsimmons Army Hospital in Aurora, Colorado on July 15, 1953 just a month after being wounded. I was to remain at Fitz until I was retired on December 31, 1955 with a 60% disability. As I was nearing the end of my hospitalization I was assigned to Fort Carson in Colorado Springs to recuperate and await one final surgical procedure. That assignment was for about four months or so and was not very interesting since I was assigned to a Personnel Center. I did luck out again and got the job as coach of the Ft. Carson rifle team.

Fitzsimmons was an excellent hospital with outstanding care. One good thing about my time there was that between surgeries I had many convalescent leaves or could live in a BOQ. In all I had fourteen surgeries including two bone grafts and a lot of other repairs. It took a lot of time and the result was I had a hand on the end of my arm instead of a hook. It is not very useful but looks far better than any artificial one.

In all, in spite of the trauma my five years in the army were rewarding and have provided many good memories. Most who have had similar experiences tend to remember the good or unusual and forget most of the bad. This is how it is with me.

21

**Kansas Woman-Owned
Business of the Year
2003**

Manufacturing Firm

Presented to

Little Ol' Cookie House
Little River, Kansas

By the

**Office of Minority & Women
Business Development**

KANSAS
DEPARTMENT *of* COMMERCE
Business Development Division

22

23

2130 Sun.
1, July '45

Dear folks,

Have received 4 letters from you now, 3 were forwarded from
New Guinea & one was in answer to my new address. Have received no
packages or Readers Digests Magazines & newspapers come 3rd class
regardless of how you send them. Keep sending those packages. I'll
get them eventually. Send the same old things-Gillette blue blades-
Cd soup & fruit, tootsie rolls & lots of Kodak 35, magazines, (Plus
X on Kodachrome) There should be 36 shots in the plus X magazines &
about 20 in the Kodachrome ones. It's unusual film so I figured you
could get it & you confirmed that. It's really not as expensive as the
others because you get 36 pictures out of each magazine. They are small,
but it's a good camera & we can enlarge them. I'd like for you to see
the country I've been in after I get home. Am trying to get some good
shots of the various places our bombers hit and if I can I'll have along
story to tell you about them along with the pictures. When there aren't
too many fighters around we go in close enough to see the bombs hit.
Several times when planes have ditched because of various reasons, our
ships are in the water before they hit. The other day a B-24 ditched &
we got all 11 men. One of 'em didn't even get wet. The fighter pilots
are our biggest worry. The weather around here is bad & they never know
just where they are. Over water work calls for a great deal of precision
& they have lots of other things to worry about. There are many islands
too but that's as much danger as it is a help. An island 10 miles long
is likely to have a peak 6000' high on it & many are active volcanoes.
We get instrument time on nearly every flight & sometimes for hours
on end you can't see your own wing tips. This obscures the islands &
you know the rest. The other day we flew at 12000' due to a 9153'
mountain. Were on instruments for 2½ hours & when we broke out of the
soup the darn thing was about 5 miles to our right and was every bit
of 11000' high. Couldn't take the lower route because of Jap fighter
strips & ack ack. The maps are all very poor & none of the country
has been surveyed, so we take every precation we can. It cost the
taxpayer about $25,000.00 to pick up a P-38 pilot the other day. He
radioed in that he was about out of gas & was going down. A B-24 circled
him until we could get there. The 24 Navigators gave us a position 150
miles in error for which there was no excuse. The meathead could see land from
where he was. The CO took his P-38 & we had a B-17 & a cat out too. We found
him, the 17 dropped him a boat ($10,000 worth). Well the parachute acted
as a sea anchor & he drifted away and couldn't get to it. We made a pass
at him in the cat, but the water was too rough to land. On the meantime
one of our rescue boats & a destroyer were racing for him. The rescue
boat won & picked him up. Then the next day we had to go back out & tow
the boat that we'd dropped back home. We're always careful to destroy all
life rafts & etc. they cost a lot of dough & have all kinds of food
water & equipment in them. The Nips and natives like to get them. It's
cost us many an unnecessary trip because some native got hold of a signaling
mirror someplace. They don't mean any harm, but just like to see the airplanes. Guess I'd better close for now. Don't worry about me if I don't
write. I flew 70 hours in 7 days awhile back. Now have 89½ hours combat
time & now have 515 rescued men to our credit (PBY's alone). Could you send
me some Mexican bill for my Short Snortes? Have 10 more letters to answer

Your son   Lytle

24

25

National Archives & Records Administration
War Department Files

2 LT Lytle R. Walker, Jr.

ID: O2082174
Branch of Service: U.S. Army
Hometown: El Paso County, TX
Status: KIA

26

Lytle R. Walker, Jr.

ID: **02082174**
Entered the Service From: **Texas**
Rank: **Second Lieutenant**

Service: **U.S. Army Air Forces, 2nd Rescue Squadron**

Died: **Saturday, January 05, 1946**
Memorialized at: **Manila American Cemetery**
Location: **Fort Bonifacio, Manila, Philippines**

Awards: **Air Medal with Oak Leaf Cluster**

27